Foreword

If you love Disney's Animal Kingdom (DAK), and hope to delve into its deepest secrets and transformations over the years, the fortune you seek is in these pages.

Chuck Schmidt dug deep into our DAK Imagineering team memories and gathered a treasure trove of personal stories about building this one-of-a-kind park. Starting with its sometimes bumpy conception, Chuck's narrative will take you through changes in DAK's offerings over the last 20 years, all the way to its latest addition of Pandora: The World of Avatar, the park's newest and greatest land, elevating the art and science of theme park experience to a new level of excellence.

Chuck got us to spill some great stories; how could we resist a seasoned journalist-turned-writer-turned-blogger who admits that he is "Goofy about Disney"? His popular blog under that playful name is a landmark among Disney fans.

So why am I the one telling you this? Great adventures start with being in the right place at the right time. In late 1989, I was a rookie Imagineer and one of only three female concept designers at Walt Disney Imagineering (WDI) in Glendale, California. Marty Sklar, then president of WDI and my mentor, sent a memo to all designers requesting quick blue-sky ideas for a new, top-secret project about animals.

Animals, real or imaginary, were the one thing I was goofy about. Or rather, deeply passionate about: as a young girl in communist Poland, I dreamt of traveling to exotic places to walk with wild animals. By chance and luck, I became the first designer, and one of the dreamers and doers, who Imagineered and built Disney's Animal Kingdom. Joe Rohde, with the blessings of Marty Sklar, Michael Eisner, and Frank Wells, led our team where no zoo or animal attraction had ever gone before.

Chuck's book brought back memories of our nearly nine years of hard work and wild adventures to make DAK happen:

smoky air of the dung and straw shelters of the Maasai; vibrant colors of the huts of Oaxacan artists; the noise of Nepal's dusty Kathmandu streets. I recalled the stench of dead elephant we saw in Tanzania's thicket before the poachers found it, and my lonely morning walk with wild animals on our first trip to Kenya, in Africa (four years later at the foot of Mount Kilimanjaro I told my team that I was expecting my second child).

Our journey had soaring highs and deepest lows, but it was worth every risk taken, including a surprise visit to Disney's CEO and CFO with a live tiger on a small leash. What better way to prove that close encounters with animals change people, including everyone that has ever worked on or visited this marvelous park. DAK continues to spread real-world magic far beyond Disney. It set new standards of captive animal care, and it expanded the frontiers of conservation programs, awareness, and research worldwide. Those ripples of influence may turn out to be the most important long-term legacy of Disney's Animal Kingdom.

Chuck Schmidt is the perfect guide for this literary safari. His ease of storytelling, deep knowledge, and lifetime of dedication to the subject, paired with his supreme journalistic fact-finding skills, make this book a uniquely entertaining and engaging journey.

Walt Disney once said, "Our greatest natural resource is the minds of our children," and "I don't like formal gardens. I like wild nature. It's just the wilderness instinct in me, I guess." Love of animals and wilderness starts with a child's mind: goofy enthusiasm and unbridled curiosity. Our growing environmental challenges and the threat of animal extinctions will require that unbridled enthusiasm, curiosity, dedication, and hard work to protect our animal friends and wilderness as the greatest natural resource for our children's children.

Thank you for your E-ticket DAK story, Chuck. All aboard and enjoy the ride!

Zofia Kostyrko
November 2017

DISNEY'S ANIMAL KINGDOM

An Unofficial History

CHUCK SCHMIDT

Foreword by Zofia Kostyrko
Former Senior Concept Designer
Walt Disney Imagineering

Theme Park Press
The Happiest Books on Earth
www.ThemeParkPress.com

Theme Park Press publishes its books in a variety of print and electronic formats. Some content that appears in one format may not appear in another.

Editor: Bob McLain
Layout: Artisanal Text

ISBN 978-1-68390-113-6
Printed in the United States of America

Theme Park Press | www.ThemeParkPress.com
Address queries to bob@themeparkpress.com

Contents

Foreword   v

Author's Note   vii

Introduction   ix

Chapter One
Gestation of a Theme Park
1

Chapter Two
In Search of Authenticity
11

Chapter Three
Plants and Animals
29

Chapter Four
Opening Day
47

Chapter Five
Safari Village / Discovery Island
57

Chapter Six
Africa
71

Chapter Seven
Conservation Station
81

Chapter Eight
DinoLand U.S.A.
87

Chapter Nine
Asia
93

Chapter Ten
Camp Minnie-Mickey
103

Chapter Eleven
Animal Kingdom Attractions Never Built
107

Chaper Twelve
Animal Kingdom Lodge
113

Chapter Thirteen
Animal Kingdom at Night
121

Chapter Fourteen
Pandora: The World of Avatar
125

Chapter Fifteen
Extracurricular Activities
137

Chapter Sixteen
Wild About Animal Kingdom
143

Acknowledgments   163
About the Author   165
About Theme Park Press   167

Author's Note

I attended the press event in conjunction with the grand opening of Disney's Animal Kingdom. That event, on April 21, 1998, was filled with pomp and ceremony...and a suitcase full of materials supplied by Walt Disney World's press and publicity department geared to help in my reporting. Back then, everything was on paper. Since I rarely throw out anything, especially when it involves Disney, I was able to dig up those media guides and materials and reference them during my research for this book. The Animal Kingdom-related periodicals and magazines in my collection were useful as well. I also was in the park when it opened to the public the following day.

Among the books I've referenced:

Dream It! Do It! and *One Little Spark!* by Marty Sklar; *Designing Disney* by John Hench; *The Making of Disney's Animal Kingdom* by Melody Malmberg; *Imagineering Field Guide to Animal Kingdom* by the Imagineers, and *Remembering Roy E. Disney* by Dave Bossert.

In addition, press events over the years centered around Animal Kingdom's growth and development—the opening of Expedition Everest, the expansion of Harambe Village, the Rivers of Light preview, and the debut of Pandora: The World of Avatar—helped enrich my knowledge of the park and ultimately served to inspire me to write this book. To that end, I'd like to thank Rick Sylvain, Michelle Baumann, the late Charlie Ridgway, and all the folks in WDW's press and publicity department for their assistance over the years.

Introduction

Whenever the creative minds in the Walt Disney Company embark on a challenging new project, they are faced with a rather daunting task: how does Disney outdo...*Disney*?

Late in 1989, then Disney chairman and CEO Michael Eisner tasked the members of Walt Disney Imagineering—the men and women responsible for bringing seemingly pie-in-the-sky ideas to fruition—to come up with a new theme park at Walt Disney World. Eisner wasn't talking about just another new amusement enterprise, however. He was aiming for something different, something that had never been attempted before. He wanted a new *species* of theme park, blending theme park entertainment with animal encounters and, perhaps most importantly, a strong message of conservation.

Disney's Animal Kingdom, which opened on April 22, 1998, was the fourth theme park built on Walt Disney World's vast 28,000-plus acre property in central Florida. It was perhaps WDW's most complex and ambitious undertaking, if only because it would be based on the compelling—and always unpredictable—world of animals. Following the rousing success of the Magic Kingdom (which opened in 1971), Epcot (1982), and Disney's Hollywood Studios (which opened in 1989 as Disney/MGM Studios), many people wondered whether a park based solely on creatures—the living, the extinct, and the mythical—could have a place in the nation's No. 1 vacation destination.

According to Joe Rohde, the chief architect of Animal Kingdom and by far its biggest cheerleader, there was never any doubt. Just prior to the park's opening, he said:

> This is a park about our love of animals. We have live animals spread out through wonderful, huge habitats as far as the eye can see...prehistoric animals lurking in the darkness...it's the whole world of animals brought to you as only Disney can.

Disney's Animal Kingdom, which turns 20 on April 22, 2018, stepped squarely into the spotlight in a big way in the spring of 2017 with the opening of Pandora: The World of Avatar, a new land devoted to celebrating the 2009 blockbuster movie *Avatar*. It was the largest, most ambitious—and easily the most popular—expansion in the park's history.

Pandora has drawn rave reviews and dramatically raised attendance at Animal Kingdom, which for years had the unenviable reputation of being a "half-day park," meaning guests felt they could experience most of what they surmised the park had to offer in about a half day before moving on to another park. In fact, during slow seasons, Animal Kingdom would be open only from 9 a.m. to 5 p.m. Pandora was the final piece of a years-long effort to reinvent Animal Kingdom and make it more enticing to park-goers, particularly during the evening hours. The addition of the Expedition Everest roller-coaster in 2006 gave Animal Kingdom a signature thrill ride; initiatives such as the Rivers of Light show, a sunset safari, and a projection display on the park's icon, the Tree of Life, have given guests a valid excuse to stick around well after the sun goes down.

The new *Avatar*-themed land is located in a section of Animal Kingdom once occupied by Camp Minnie-Mickey, a rustic meet-and-greet area where guests young and old could pose with Disney characters in a summer camp-like setting. Also featured in Camp Minnie-Mickey was Festival of the Lion King and Pocahontas and her Forest Friends, two live stage shows.

To make room for Pandora (which occupies 12 acres and features two new, innovative attractions—Na'vi River Journey and Avatar: Flight of Passage, as well as a bioluminescent land-scape and floating mountains, all cornerstones of the movie), Festival of the Lion King was moved to a new venue near Harambe Village in the Africa section of the park. The rest of Camp Minnie-Mickey, having outlived its usefulness, simply faded into Disney parks lore.

Animal Kingdom is located on the southwest portion of the Walt Disney World property, just north of U.S. Route 192. To reach the park by car or bus from other sections of the property, guests drive south along the Osceola Parkway. As they approach the park, the man-made Tree of Life, the snow-covered peaks of Expedition Everest, and now Pandora's floating mountains are clearly visible above the treetops. About a mile past the park's entrance sits Animal Kingdom Lodge, a spectacular African-inspired resort which is a visual masterpiece and blends seamlessly with the entire area's theming. Like the theme park it adjoins, Animal Kingdom Lodge—divided into Kidani Village and Jambo House—brings guests thisclose to a stunning array of exotic animals. It is common for guests staying in rooms with a savannah view to awake in the morning, open their blinds, and see giraffe or zebra or wildebeests grazing right outside their balconies. There also are observation decks located off the two resorts' lobbies that afford guests the opportunity to get even closer to the animal action. Like the theme park, most of Animal Kingdom Lodge's animal population was obtained from North American zoos accredited by the Association of Zoos and Aquariums.

When Animal Kingdom, some of the advertising pitches included "Disney's imagination gone wild" and "nah-ta-zu," which was a clever way of saying Animal Kingdom was "not a zoo." Even though Animal Kingdom has one of the largest collection of birds, reptiles, and animals on the planet, it is very much atypical of a zoo. You'll never see animals confined in a traditional sense; they roam wild and free in meticulously recreated natural habitats, under the watchful eye of many skilled animal keepers.

In fact, Eisner went to great lengths to make sure Animal Kingdom would never be perceived as just a zoo. "Michael Eisner really pushed us to make sure we were telling *stories* about animals," said Marty Sklar, who was the creative leader of Walt Disney Imagineering when the idea of an animal-themed theme park was first proposed. Animal Kingdom "had to be as far removed from a zoo as possible," he added.

The first inkling to the outside world about this "new species of theme park" came in 1995, when the Disney Channel ran a series of spots announcing plans to build what was briefly known as *Wild* Animal Kingdom in Walt Disney World. The wheels for the project had begun turning some five years before that, in late 1989. Construction commenced two months after the first public announcements, in August 1995. After the project was unveiled, a scale model of Animal Kingdom was put on display off Town Square in the Magic Kingdom to further whet the appetites of Disney park guests.

In announcing the new park, Eisner said:

> Disney recognizes that the need for awareness of endangered animals and their environments never has been greater. We believe that, as storytellers and communicators, we are in a unique position to promote a deeper understanding and love for all animals. We hope that people will come here because they love animals and that, when they leave, they will have a new knowledge and respect for the beauty and complexity of the animal kingdom.

The site chosen for Animal Kingdom was far off the beaten path in relation to Walt Disney World's three other theme parks, two water parks, most of the resorts, and the shopping/dining/entertainment district now known as Disney Springs. Marty Sklar told a story about just how remote the Animal Kingdom property is:

> When we were building Epcot, we needed massive amounts of dirt to fill some areas of the park, so we had to "borrow" dirt from someplace else on the property. I told the crews to find a place that was so far off the beaten path that there was no chance we'd ever build anything on it. That place turned out to be where we built Animal Kingdom!

Other than being used as a dirt borrow pit for Epcot, the Animal Kingdom site also was used as an area where new fireworks shows were tested—it was that out of the way.

Animal Kingdom's remoteness (it's about a 20-minute ride from the Magic Kingdom and is not accessible by either boat or monorail, unlike the other three parks) lends itself perfectly to its faraway, exotic nature. When walking around the park, you truly feel as if you've been transported to another place, another time. And, with the opening of Pandora, you get the distinct feeling you've been transported to another world as well.

Animal Kingdom will always hold a special place in my heart. Unlike Marty, who proudly held the distinction of having been at the grand openings of all 12 Disney theme parks worldwide, Animal Kingdom is the only Disney park I attended on its opening day. With that in mind, this book will explore what those first wide-eyed guests encountered when they entered the park on April 22, 1998, and what guests experience today after the park's nearly 20-year maturation. In addition, we'll look at just what it took to bring this unique and remarkable theme park experience to life. Much like all living beings, Animal Kingdom was conceived, was born, and struggled through growing pains before ultimately finding its place in the world...in this case, Walt Disney World.

CHAPTER ONE

Gestation of a Theme Park

Walt Disney was a man of many talents, from artist, to movie mogul, to theme park creator, to businessman, to television advocate (yes, back in the 1950s there were many people who thought TV was just a fad). He also was every bit a riverboat gambler, willing to risk literally everything he owned on ideas that seemed to make little or no sense...at least to everyone but him. Among his many interests outside his business world was a love of the animals with whom we share planet Earth.

As Walt once said, "Some of the most fascinating people I've ever met were animals." Indeed, animals and birds, rodents and reptiles, were always the stars of Disney's animated works, from the myriad forest creatures in *Snow White and the Seven Dwarfs*, to the *Jungle Book*'s swingin' menagerie, to elephants flying in *Dumbo*, or the spotted puppies in *101 Dalmatians*. Disney's first Audio-Animatronics show saw dozens of singing and talking birds come to life in the Enchanted Tiki Room. And, of course, there was the little guy who started it all, Mickey Mouse. But in 1947, Walt decided to step away from animated creatures and get real. He gave the green light to a project that would ultimately offer rare insight into the heretofore largely ignored world of animals: a series of film documentaries that told the stories of a variety of species in the wild—where they were born, how they lived, how they hunted (or were hunted), how they procreated, how they survived nature's wrath, and how they died. In a very real sense, these films showcased the great circle of life, a subject broached so aptly in another of Disney's animal-themed animated classics, *The Lion King*.

When Walt contracted filmmakers Alfred and Elma Milotte to head to Alaska's Priloilot Islands to capture wild animals in their natural habitats, his company was embarking on a decades-long journey that would ultimately educate, inform, and entertain people. Through his True-Life Adventures series (and, in recent years, the Disneynature series), Walt gave his audience an intimate view of animals—untamed, in the wild—that few humans had ever witnessed before.

The end product of the Milottes' work in Alaska was *Seal Island*, a half-hour documentary that was released in 1948. Like many of the projects he championed throughout his life, Walt faced stiff opposition from "the experts" when it came time to screen the film in theaters. And like all the other projects where he faced unyielding naysayers, Walt eventually triumphed. Walt convinced a friend who owned the Crown Theater in Pasadena, California, to screen *Seal Island* for a week, thus qualifying it for Academy Award consideration. *Seal Island* went on to win an Academy Award in 1949 for Best Documentary, validating Walt's belief in the project. In total, there were 14 True-Life Adventures, eight of which won Oscars during the series' run from 1948–1960.

The True-Life Adventures (TLA) kick-started a company-wide focus on conservationism, an initiative that has permeated the Walt Disney Company to this day and has manifested itself in various ways. In fact, many historians refer to the True-Life Adventures as a catalyst for the entire worldwide conservation movement. Roy E. Disney, Walt's nephew who cut his teeth with the company producing many of the TLA films, called that a "fortunate by-product" of the series' success. He told Vacation Magic magazine in 2006:

> Back then, we didn't even know what ecology meant. But we knew how to entertain people, and that's what we set out to do with those films.

Over the years, the philosophy espoused by Roy E. Disney has become known as "edu-tainment" within Disney circles: educating, while entertaining.

It was Roy E. Disney, according to Dave Bossert, the author of *Remembering Roy E. Disney*, the definitive biography of the man who was so influential in the rebirth of Disney animation in the 1980s, who first broached the subject of an animal-themed theme park. Bossert wrote:

> Yes, the Animal Kingdom park was really created because of Roy's urging and the connection that the company had had to all of the nature films, including the True-Life Adventures series. The park started at the suggestion of Roy. Roy had a very firm, behind-the-scenes way of getting things done.

Marty Sklar concurred:

> Roy Disney was deeply involved in the park, mostly through the advisory board. He really helped us in putting together the board because they were all familiar with what Roy had done with the True-Life Adventures. [His involvement] was very helpful in using his name and his aura, if you will.
>
> [The members of the advisory board] were really good because they were very direct with us. When we were making mistakes or we were going off in directions that were not appropriate or were inaccurate, they weren't shy about telling us.

In the years following Animal Kingdom's opening until his death in 2009, Roy visited the park whenever he was in Florida. "Roy absolutely loved the Animal Kingdom park and went to it every chance he got," Bossert wrote. When a DVD retrospective of the True-Life Adventures series was in the works, with Roy as the narrator, much of the filming took place at Animal Kingdom, allowing him to visit several behind-the-scenes locales in the park to witness veterinarians treating animals.

Roy said:

> Animals and the natural world are as important to the legacy of the Walt Disney Company as Snow White and Mickey Mouse.

In the early 1950s, when Walt was dreaming of building Disneyland, a place where parents and children could have fun together, he had an idea for an attraction that would bring animals and humans together. Early concepts for the Jungle Cruise called for the use of live animals stationed along the banks of the river as boatloads of passengers floated by.

According to Marty Sklar:

> [The genesis of Animal Kingdom] went all the way back to the Jungle Cruise. One of Walt's early ideas was to create an attraction with real animals, but he realized that the animals would be asleep half the time. There were other reasons to be wary of doing something like that, because PETA [People for the Ethical Treatment of Animals] was so aggressive at that time about captured animals. They had a lot of issues with zoos and private collections of animals.

In the end, the idea of live animals along the Jungle Cruise was scrapped in favor of dozens of audio-animatronic figures, positioned either on the shorelines or in the waterways. But that didn't stop the company from putting the idea of some type of major animal-themed attraction on a back-burner, to be resurrected in the future.

Conservation—both for animals and native vegetation—was a cornerstone of Disney's philosophy when it was making the move to central Florida. During the planning stages of Walt Disney World, more than one-quarter of the vast central Florida property (about the size of the city of San Francisco) was set aside as a permanent wildlife preservation area. It was Walt Disney himself who personally initiated the establishment of a 7,500-acre conservation area within Walt Disney World's initial land purchase of 28,000 acres. That area has grown to more than 8,300 acres, pristine land to be left forever in its natural state. Florida's native species—including ospreys, bald eagles, tortoises, and deer—were the chief benefactors. The area also serves as a place for migratory birds to rest their weary wings each season. Another key component of Disney's conservation efforts was to be as "kind" to the land as possible. During the early phases of construction, Sklar said:

> The Army Corps of Engineers in the beginning were digging drainage canals in a straight line. It was [Imagineer] John Hench who was responsible for the snake-like, curving drainage canals that followed the natural contours of the land.

As early as the 1960s, when Disney was gearing to move to central Florida, it began a program dubbed "environmentality," which combined recycling and innovative waste-water systems with environmental education and conservation. It became part of the company's corporate culture. Disney initiated forward-thinking programs in recycling, composting, and water conservation. It even replaced plastic bubble wrap for guest purchases with a packing product that is made from 100% recycled cardboard.

An example of Disney's commitment to "environmentality" came during the construction phase at Animal Kingdom, when work crews took great pains to have as little impact on the environment as possible. Outside the park proper, a bridge needed to be built across Reedy Creek to allow vehicles to go from the Osceola Parkway to the parking lot. The problem was, that bridge would have to be constructed in an environmentally sensitive wetland. The solution? Build the 1,000-foot bridge from the *top down*, rather than the more traditional *bottom up*. A temporary work platform was erected, keeping construction vehicles from chewing up the surrounding precious land. They took that philosophy a step further by substituting vegetable oil for hydraulic fluid in the heavy equipment, ensuring that if a spill did occur, it would have less of an environmental impact.

The project manager, John Kennedy, said:

> This was the first time a bridge of this type was built at Disney. For a bridge, this is a showcase piece.

Animal Kingdom wasn't Disney's first effort to create an animal-friendly park with an eye toward the environment, education, and conservation. A few years after Walt Disney World opened in 1971, guests could take a short boat ride from the dock at the Contemporary Resort, across Bay Lake, to a place originally called Blackbeard's Island (later renamed Discovery Island), where a 11.5-acre zoological park featuring 200 species of wildlife—including a massive Galapagos turtle, lemurs, wallabies, flamingos, swans, alligators, and lizards—entertained and educated visitors. There was a 2,700-square-foot animal hospital on the island with a full-time vet on duty. Discovery Island was an accredited member of the Association of Zoos and Aquariums and was involved in breeding programs for endangered species. As it turned out, Discovery Island portended of bigger things to come at Walt Disney World, animal-wise.

Among the many animal-themed experiences available to guests when Walt Disney World opened was the Tri-Circle D Ranch at the Fort Wilderness Campground. On the ranch was a petting zoo and stables for the horses who are integral members of the WDW cast. Today, there are some 80 to 90 horses housed in modern, state-of-the-art stables. They serve a variety of functions in the park, such as pulling the Main Street trolley, accompanying a princess-themed coach for a Fairytale Wedding, even carrying the Headless Horseman during Mickey's Not So Scary Halloween Party. They also are available for guests to take leisurely horseback rides through the campground's winding, wooded trails.

When Epcot opened in 1981, The Living Seas was among the featured attractions in the Future World section of the park and took up the mantle of marine science and environmental education. A 5.7-million-gallon salt water tank was the focal point of The Living Seas, where sharks, sea turtles, and bottle-nose dolphins joined nearly 3,000 fish in a cornucopia of flourishing marine life. Emphasis was placed on animal management techniques and research, as well as coral reef ecology. Florida's endangered manatees are among the many sea creatures that receive special attention at The Living Seas.

And at The Land pavilion in Epcot, an innovative integrated pest management program was introduced to eradicate insect pests and plant diseases on greenhouse crops without the use of harsh chemicals. Among the strategies: place "good bugs" in the greenhouse who naturally devour the "bad bugs."

To this day, Disney remains committed to animal conservation. To wit: For the past 10 years, Disney has held what it calls the Tour de Turtles event. In 2017, in conjunction with the Sea Turtle Conservancy, two female loggerhead turtles were released from Disney's Vero Beach Resort along Florida's east coast. The turtles were tagged with satellite transmitters and were tracked during their swim to foraging grounds, an aqua journey that might reach thousands of miles. The turtles are always given Disney character names: in 2017, they were named Cruz and Sally, characters from the new *Cars 3* movie. Each year, a large crowd gathers to watch as the plucky turtles make their way from the sandy shores into the water.

Since 1995, the Disney Conservation Fund has been an important vessel in the Disney company's efforts to protect the planet and help kids develop lifelong conservation values. Included in its mission is to support the study of wildlife; protect habitats; develop community conservation and education programs in critical ecosystems; and promote experiences that connect children to nature across the globe.

Finally, about 30 minutes away from Walt Disney World, at the headwaters of the Florida everglades ecosystem, sits the Nature Conservancy's Disney Wilderness Preserve, a nearly 12,000-acre sanctuary. Both the Walt Disney Company and the Nature Conservancy partnered with other ecology-minded groups to help bring the once environmentally sensitive area back to life.

Disney executive Jerry Montgomery said:

> We are incredibly proud of the relationship we've developed with the Nature Conservancy. Our company's focus on the environment goes back to Walt himself. This relationship with the Nature Conservancy has created a conservation and sustainability model that has been replicated around the world.

According to the group's website:

> The Disney Wilderness Preserve near Kissimmee stands as a testament not only to Disney's words, but to the power of cooperation, perseverance, and innovative thinking.

In 1989, with the Walt Disney Company fully involved in the construction of its first-ever European theme park in Marne-la-Vallee outside of Paris, France, Michael Eisner gave the go-ahead to tap into the company's rich animal and conservation legacy and Disney's Animal Kingdom was launched.

Eisner said:

> This is to the traditional zoo as the motion picture was to the stage play. A leap forward that keeps the concept

of combining education and entertainment alive and
well. The need for awareness of endangered animals and
their environments has never been greater. We are in
a unique position to promote deeper understanding and
love for all animals.

Once Eisner gave the green light, Marty Sklar got the word
out to the company's artists and designers, seeking their
input for the animal-themed project. From those volunteers,
a small group of Walt Disney Imagineering's most creative
minds, headed by self-proclaimed "long-haired hippie type"
Joe Rohde, was then tasked with bringing the boss' broad
vision into focus. Eisner made it clear that he wanted to build
a new theme park on Walt Disney World property, but not
just another ride-and-show venue. He wanted to explore the
possibility of building a unique theme park, one that would
enlighten, educate, and inspire guests. It would be a venue
based on the broad spectrum of Earth's creatures—past,
present, and mythological.

In a tradition that dates back to Herb Ryman's first drawing
of Disneyland in 1953, Rohde painted a concept aerial overview
in 1991 of his vision for Animal Kingdom. As with any concept
art, the painting wasn't so much what *would* be built, as what
could be built. Close inspection of the work shows elaborately
themed villages surrounded by waterways and connected by
foot bridges. There were plenty of trees, as well as a vast, open
savannah. Interestingly, there was a snow-peaked mountain,
perhaps a portent of Expedition Everest more than 15 years
later. At the entrance, Rohde painted a replica of Noah's ark.

He said:

> The research that goes into these parks is not merely
> research into the real world. It is research into the great
> works of art of all those who have come before. That's
> how it works. This is art.

But as the project began to take shape, CEO Eisner and
Disney company president Frank Wells began to have second
thoughts. They started to doubt whether a theme park based
on animals would generate enough excitement among Disney
guests...and, by extension, a profit.

According to Marty Sklar:

> At one point, Michael and Frank got really nervous about whether animals were really going to be that much of an attraction. That's when we had that meeting where Joe brought the tiger in.

Joe Rohde managed to commandeer a live Bengal tiger and had it brought into the meeting of top Disney execs, where the fate of the project may well have hung in the balance. He began the meeting by telling the bosses: "We know that there are concerns about whether animals are, in and of themselves, dramatic." A few minutes later, the 400-pound female tiger was led into the room by her keeper. Rohde kept talking while the execs seemed to collectively cringe in fear. "Yes, there's an element of danger" with animals, Rohde added, "but that's necessary for drama."

Marty Sklar admitted he was a tad weak in the knees at the sight of the orange, black-striped big cat striding around the room:

> I don't think I was as scared as Frank Wells was. But it was a key moment, because you're in a meeting where the discussion is about if animals will be a big enough draw, and all of a sudden, this full-sized tiger is in the room with you. That made a BIG impression.

Now satisfied that animals *would* have a lasting, powerful impact, the Walt Disney Company went full-speed ahead with the development of the new park. It would be an animal-themed park, yes...but definitely nah-ta-zu.

CHAPTER TWO
In Search of Authenticity

Joe Rohde said:

> In February of 1990, a small group of Imagineers sat in the smallest conference room in the smallest trailer on the Walt Disney Imagineering lot. I was among those few people leading development of a new concept for a park in Florida. It had to be something completely different from any animal park in the world—different from any theme park we or anyone else had ever created.

The very first meeting about the park was conducted in August of 1989. It lasted five minutes. According to Rohde:

> Michael Eisner said, "People like animals. People like Disney. If Disney does something with animals, people will come." I said, "OK, there's the mission."

At that point, however, the idea of Animal Kingdom was a "dark-horse kind of project." Euro Disneyland was well underway, and Eisner's highly touted Disney Decade, where the company would expand its footprint in the parks, resorts, animated films—even into the unchartered waters of operating its own cruise line—was in full swing as the 1990s unfolded.

Although Rohde was tasked with leading the Animal Kingdom project, it wasn't as if there were a long line of Imagineers yearning to take up the challenge.

Rohde admitted years later:

> The only reason a junior designer like me got the assignment was that nobody else really wanted it. They figured it would be just a zoo and likely not get done, which had a really good chance of being true.

There also was the issue of a 400-page white paper study that had been conducted about zoos in America, which concluded that an animal-themed park might not be such a great idea.

Even though the Animal Kingdom project stumbled out of the starting gate, Rohde's team came up with a clear theme for this new theme park venture. A "theme," according to Rohde, is the underlying value system on which a story is built. The new park's theme would encompass "the intrinsic value of nature." With that as a reference point, all the myriad decisions involved in designing and developing the park would follow. The first big decision was the most obvious: picking a site.

The land chosen for this new park, off the beaten path when compared to the Magic Kingdom, Epcot, and the Disney/MGM Studios, was "500 acres of unremarkable palmetto and scrub oaks, a former cow pasture without any contour," Rohde said. "When I first saw the site, I was truly terrified"...not too unlike the way the first Disney executives reacted in the mid-1960s as they flew over central Florida to get a first glance at the entire 28,000-acre Walt Disney World property.

Rohde described the first time he walked the Animal Kingdom site:

> [It was] just sand. Miles and miles of sand. The first time I went out there, it looked like Mongolia. Nothing but sand dunes. I felt like Lawrence of Arabia.

Rohde became disoriented during his walk and ended up getting lost. The sand, however, was a perfect place to build this park, because it offered excellent drainage for the foliage that eventually would be planted there.

Rohde wasn't alone in the quest to turn this "unremarkable" acreage into a living, breathing, functioning environment. Writer Kevin Brown (Rohde's roommate at Occidental College), designer Zofia Kostyrko, associate producer Patsy Tillisch, Christopher West, and Tony Marando comprised the initial design team. That group would soon expand with the additions of landscaper Paul Comstock, show designer John Shields, concept architect Tom Sze, producer Ann Malmlund, park designer Kelley Ford, and Eric Eberhart of WDW Operations. Their quest was daunting, dangerous, exhilarating, exhausting, rewarding, and ultimately, wildly successful. Team members would spend countless hours planning, thousands and thousands of miles traveling the world, and months away from home nurturing the dream of a theme park based on the world of animals.

The figurative foundation for the park was poured during those first months in that tiny trailer in the WDI lot. There were daily brainstorming sessions, where ideas would be bounced back and forth as if each member was playing verbal ping pong.

Landscape architect Paul Comstock recalled:

> We were in the funkiest trailer. It was an old, beat-up thing and you'd walk through it and the floor would squeak, and we'd be sitting around a table—Joe, Zofia, myself, and a few others, just tossing around ideas. You'd say that this idea involves X and everyone would say, "Oh, that's a pretty good idea." There could be this...and it could be a boat ride...and if it's a boat ride, it could have this...If it was a roller-coaster, it would have this and it could go through that.

> It was almost like improvisational jazz. I was trained to be a musician, and after you learn all your scales, when you sit with other musicians you can kind of play off an idea...the horn player plays a riff, followed by the bass player...they play off each other. It would go around the room in circles, crossing back and forth.

The Imagineers in those meetings ended up making beautiful music together.

So many elements came in to play during those early design meetings, heretofore unexplored by previous theme park designers but crucial to the success of an animal-themed park. How does one create a flourishing forest—where guests could trudge through an exploration trail and view animals in natural habitats—on that barren, open pasture? How do you craft animal habitats that a wide variety of species would accept as their home? What type of shows and attractions would fit into this mélange of ideas? How does one go about building a vast, realistic African savannah where guests can observe animals walking freely in an open, natural environment? And just how do you construct an entire African village that looks and feels as realistic as if it had been lifted—lock, stock, and baobab tree—from the East African seaside to central Florida? The answer, in every case, was research. Boots-on-the-ground research.

In addition, the team was faced with the hard, cold fact that—unlike a regular theme park, where the gates are closed at the end of the night, the lights are turned off, and everyone goes home—animals need constant care, 24 hours a day, seven days a week, every day of the year. Not only that, but all the animals to be housed in the park would have different nutritional needs; the more exotic the species, the more limited the food choices. And larger animals, such as elephants, tend to be voracious eaters.

Perhaps the most significant—and least-known—aspect of Animal Kingdom during its design and development stage was the formation of an advisory committee to lend its expertise to the project.

Marty Sklar said:

> Because of our experience with advisory boards on Epcot [they helped in many ways, from advice that kept us out of trouble story-wise to opening doors to people because of the board members' know-how and friendships], I recommended that we set up an advisory board for [the Animal Kingdom] project. It became a vital part of the development because of PETA and because there were great organizations and people represented: World Wildlife Fund; the Bronx Zoo; Zoo Atlanta; AZA [Association of Zoos and Aquariums]; Conservation International, represented by Russ Mittermeier; and the American Society for the Prevention of Cruelty to Animals [ASPCA], represented by Roger Caras.
>
> This group opened many doors and gave the project credibility.

The committee members came from the nation's finest zoos, leading educational institutions, and major conservation and wildlife foundations. The panel of experts advised Disney's Imagineers on such important topics as continuing animal care and educational programs, as well as how to blend entertainment with the important message of conservation.

The Animal Kingdom Advisory Committee consisted of Karen Allen, P. Dee Boersma, William Burnham, Roger Caras, Bill Conway, Michael Hutchins, John Lukas, Terry Maple, Ray Mendez, and Russell Mittermeier. The chairman of the board was Roy E. Disney, he of the True-Life Adventures pedigree.

Sklar continued:

> We had Bill Conway, probably the No. 1 zoo person in the country from the Bronx Zoo leading the board. [The advisory board] was really a key piece, because everybody knew the people that we had on it. And they were really terrific. They helped open some doors for us because in the zoological community, you obtain animals by trading animals. They're born in one place, but they may have too many, let's say, elephants, so they'd trade an elephant for a hippo, or whatever may be.

Of course, it's a lot more complicated than that. As part of receiving accreditation from the Association of Zoos and Aquariums [AZA], Disney was required to participate in the Species Survival Plan [SSP], a program which oversees the population management of select species within AZA member institutions. Each SSP program (there are nearly 500), is responsible, according to the AZA website, "for developing a comprehensive population studbook and a breeding and transfer plan which identifies population management goals and recommendations to ensure the sustainability of a healthy, genetically diverse and demographically varied AZA population." Sadly, some species only have a chance to continue in captivity, as their natural habitats are gone or nearly gone or their species has been hunted to or near extinction.

The board met for the first time in January of 1993. Over the years, Sklar said:

> The board members received regular updates from Disney. We had the concept meetings in California, but as the project evolved, we started having the meetings in Florida at the site...and they continued to meet after the park opened, as well.

Once word had leaked of Disney's intentions to build an animal-themed park, the eyes of the world zeroed in on the company. Would-be critics sharpened their pens, just waiting for Disney to slip up. It wasn't as if these critics didn't have reason to be skeptical. For years, many zoos and parks around the country came under sharp criticism for keeping animals in cramped cages, among other offenses.

According to Paul Comstock:

> A lot of people out there tried to stick a knife and make a hole in [our plans to develop Animal Kingdom]. We had to be clean and above-board on everything.

Previous attempts to create parks where animals were featured more often than not ended in failure. Among them was a place called Jungle Habitat in West Milford, New Jersey, which was open from 1972–1977, and where future Animal Kingdom animal-care director Rick Barongi got his start as an animal trainer during the summer months.

Barongi said:

> I worked years ago at Jungle Habitat. It was open for about five years. It was owned by Warner Brothers, who leased animals from the International Animal Exchange. I'm not sure why it folded; I guess it wasn't making a lot of money. That's where I got my first animal experience. Nobody knew what they were doing and they let you do things that nowadays they wouldn't let you do. We had to chase the rhinos in at night on foot. We'd slap them on the asses, and if they turned around, we'd run and hide behind a tree.

Animal Kingdom obtained Barongi's services to head up animal project development for the park. Jungle Habitat experience aside, Barongi had a long and impressive resume in the animal-care field when he was tapped by Disney: a bachelor's degree in biology and animal services from Cornell University, a master's degree in zoology from Rutgers University, curator of mammals for the Miami Metro Zoo and the San Diego Zoo, and director of the San Diego Children's Zoo. Under Barongi's skilled hand, Disney assembled a select group of animal experts to lend their time and talents to the arduous task of creating a place where animals would receive state-of-the-art care...and just as importantly, thrive in a man-made setting.

Barongi was working at the San Diego Zoo when he received a phone call from Patsy Tillisch, a member of Rohde's team:

> I was in San Diego one day in 1989 and the guy in the manager's office said, "There's a call from Disney that I'm forwarding to you." Patsy Tillisch was on the line [she was Joe Rohde's kind of assistant at the time] and she said, "Hey, we're doing this project. We can't tell you a lot about it, but it involves animals." She didn't tell me much, but she asked me if I could come up for a day so they could meet me.
>
> That's when I learned about the project and that's when I met Joe Rohde. The guy's incredible. Such a nice guy. The way he thinks...he's such a visionary, always looking at the big picture. I had an office next to Joe for three and a half years, so I got to know him really well.

Even though Barongi was the perfect man for the job, he wasn't Disney's first choice: the widely respected Bill Conway was Disney's preference to head up animal project development for the park.

Barongi said:

> I found out a year later that they had contacted Bill Conway from the Bronx Zoo. He had come out once to look at the project and after they offered him the job, he said, "I can't do that, I have a zoo to run," so he didn't take the job. He never told me that and neither did Disney.

Barongi started out as a consultant on the park before segueing to full-time director of Animal Operations, and finally, director of Animal Project Development. One of his first responsibilities was to recruit like-minded animal care experts to lend their expertise to the project.

> To me, it's all about the commitment of the keepers. Before the '80s and '90s, the people who worked in zoos were basically ex-military men, mostly doing it as a second job. They'd clean the cages and then disappear for the day. Then we started to get a lot of females in the profession and a lot of college-educated people. It changed from the bottom up, not from the top down. And the pressure from the animal rights community certainly forced zoos to be

more transparent because they wanted to stay out of the headlines. But they did it for the wrong reasons.

There were good zoos out there. The animal care standards were there already. Disney's Animal Kingdom did change the industry in terms of care and conservation. But what Disney really did was to connect animals to a storyline. Zoos were not connecting animals with stories in the wild. Disney was starting to do that. They support conservation like other zoos, but they'd bring in conservation people and they made celebrities out of many of these conservationists.

Barongi, working with Animal Kingdom vice president Bob Lamb, a long-time animal-rights advocate himself, recruited some of the country's top curators, animal keepers, veterinarians, behavioral specialists, and executives from the nation's leading zoos to spearhead the effort to establish an animal-friendly, yet educational environment in a theme park setting, something that had never been done before. The group included Dr. Peregrine Wolff (Minnesota Zoo), Dr. Beth Stevens (Zoo Atlanta), Bruce Read (St. Louis Zoo), Joe Christman (Phoenix Zoo), John Lehnhardt (National Zoo, Washington, D.C.), Dr. Nancy Pratt (San Diego Zoo), Connie Philipp (Memphis Zoo), Grenville Roles (Tracy Aviary, Salt Lake City, Utah), Dr. Jill Mellen (Portland, Oregon, Zoo), Marty Sevenich (Brookfield, Illinois, Zoo), Dr. Jackie Ogden (San Diego Zoo), and Kathryn Lehnhardt (National Zoo).

Joe Rohde was very much the conductor of this far-flung orchestra of intellectuals, experts, and advisors. It turns out he had been working up to becoming Animal Kingdom's executive designer years before the park was on the drawing board, even back to his early years growing up in Hawaii:

> I always had a collection of frogs, a rusty bathtub full of fish, and a backyard full of tropical birds for company.

After earning a liberal arts degree from Occidental College in California, he took a teaching job at a prep school in Los Angeles before landing a position at Walt Disney Imagineering in 1980. In 1985, he received his five-year Disney service pin and promptly inserted it into his freshly pierced left ear. From that day forward, Rohde has placed additional earrings and trinkets he's acquired from faraway travel destinations, places like Zanzibar and Katmandu, writing on his Instagam page:

> My ear is a celebrity. I'm like the guy walking next to the celebrity. Nobody would remember me if it wasn't for the natural history museum hanging from the side of my head.

His elongated ear lobe, weighed down by all those bobbles, makes him a rather unique individual...just the type needed to put together as unique a theme park as had ever been conceived.

Rohde's extensive travels to remote locales helped set the foundation for Animal Kingdom. In. 1987, he and his wife, Melody Malmberg, visited Bali to fulfill a lifelong dream of his. They immersed themselves in the local culture and witnessed many things, including jungle temples, natural animal habitats, and eye-opening Hindu ceremonies:

> Most tourists miss the real temple ceremonies which involve knives, fire, and animal sacrifices, but we wanted to see it all.

There followed an extended visit to Nepal in 1989, a trip filled with mountain hiking and wild animal encounters. Through it all, he made drawings—colorful huts, native costumes, regional foliage, creatures large and small, majestic mountains ranges—that would serve him well in the years ahead.

Those personal adventures set the stage for the boots-on-the-ground research trips made by Rohde and his team during the planning and development stages for Animal Kingdom.

Marty Sklar said:

> The early Imagineers who came from art direction backgrounds in the motion picture field were older and had frequently traveled widely. Joe Rohde was not just an advocate for true "boots-on-the-ground" research, he was a veteran traveler to Asia and Polynesia. Joe's belief that his team absolutely had to experience lions and elephants on a real African safari, and to travel to Asian byways far from civilization, was crucial.

Prior to Animal Kingdom's opening day, Rohde said:

> The process of creating this park has led us on adventures in nearly every corner of the globe. We have rafted whitewater rivers of the Himalayas; driven, walked, even ballooned across the African savannah; searched for fossil bones of extinct dinosaurs; and met with respected leaders in the world of conservation. The essence of these adventures is what we hope we have captured in Disney's Animal Kingdom.

Senior concept designer Zofia Kostyrko said:

> The research trips were essential for the sake of authenticity because when you design any space, you need to design a kind of kinetic feel of it and you also need to understand the texture of it, the smell of it, the light of it...all of these things make it look authentic.

The team started making research trips locally, visiting zoos across America. Added Ms. Kostyrko:

> Everybody thought that it was a joke that Disney was stepping into the world of animals, because nobody believed that we were going to take it seriously. But we knew that animals are not just entertainment, they are very emotional to a lot of people.

Ms. Kostyrko explained that the group then went to Canada and several sites in Europe, observing, taking notes, and learning, before going even further abroad:

> The first really big trip we took was to Kenya, Tanzania, and Zanzibar [in June of 1990]. It was an absolutely insane adventure with all kinds of stuff going on. It was really rugged. There was one flight, to Tanzania, where the plane was so small I think I had to sit on someone's lap. I don't think we were able to take all the luggage. We visited a tented camp with a bar inside a giant tree trunk in Tanzania that became inspiration for the baobab tree in the Africa queue. To get there, we landed on a dry river bed, the kind of landing strip that is available only during certain times of the year.
>
> Another time we were hiking in the jungle and we saw a dead elephant, which was quite sad to witness

first-hand. I did something that wasn't terribly wise, but this also speaks to being from Disney, where you think that everything is safe around you. We went to a reserve in Kenya on one of our first trips and I went for a hike in the morning outside of the compound, and I saw some buffalo in the fog and some giraffe. It was really dangerous; it would have made a nice story for my obituary. The team wasn't very happy with me. But there was such a sense of authenticity being out there with the animals. It was an incredible, incredible adventure to be able to do that. We had other close calls, hiking through the bush… getting stuck in the mud in the jungle.

On a return trip to Africa a few years later, Ms. Kostyrko had a pleasant surprise for her fellow team members:

The second time we went to Africa, I was five months pregnant. I didn't tell my team because I knew they wouldn't take me if I said anything. My doctor knew about the trip and OK'd it. But then they took us on this ride—it wasn't an E-ticket ride, it was more like a F ticket…total fear—in a Jeep. That same evening, facing Mount Kilimanjaro, I told my team that I was going to have my second baby.

The team's research trips spanned more than eight years, with members traversing some of the most remote areas of the world. During their travels, which covered more than 500,000 miles, they took photos (when taking photos was permitted), made sketches, and collected artifacts…all for the sake of authenticity and to craft an environment that was so different from anything else that had ever been created before—or after—as a theme park venue.

For the record, the team embarked on extensive research trips in June of 1990 (Kenya, Tanzania, Zanzibar); 1993 (Thailand and Nepal); 1994 (Bali, India, and Bhutan); 1995 (Mexico); and 1996 (East Africa). Subsequent trips to a variety of far-off lands also were taken by different members of the team in the years prior to opening.

Marty Sklar backed his Imagineers' quest for authenticity, but he also had to keep a watchful eye on the budget:

The research trips, I have to admit, were hugely important, and Joe insisted that his whole team go on them.
It really became a problem for us because those were
expensive trips. And there were so many of them. I used
to joke that whenever I needed to talk to Joe, he'd be
off in Africa or somewhere else in the world. It was
obvious—when you look at the park and see how authentic it is, the immersive experience that people are able to
enjoy—how important [these research trip were]. They
were absolutely essential.

One crucial aspect of the group's "adventures" was to
immerse themselves in vast African savannahs. They took
note of the contour of the land, the plant-life growing there,
the grasses and the watering holes so crucial to the animals'
survival and which types of animals lived on the savannahs.
Ultimately, they would bring back trees, shrubs, plants, and
seeds that would allow them to replicate a savannah down to
the smallest detail. "Disney was the first to build a realistic
African savannah," said Paul Comstock, the park's lead landscape designer. Long-time Disney parks landscape architect
Bill Evans, whose roots ran as far back as Disneyland and who
offered his expertise to the Animal Kingdom project, said:

We cast trees as characters into the landscape, taking
into consideration size, shade, and accent. If you can't
use your ideal tree, you look around for somebody who
can play the part. It's sort of like choosing an understudy.

Comstock recalled:

At the beginning, we would have specific environments
that we had seen during our research trips and we were
tasked with replicating them. There would be a specific
image that comes into my mind: 15 to 20 elephants, near
a river in Kenya. Mud-bank walls, verdant acacias up on
top with all these elephants drinking out of the river.
One of the iconic scenes that we would be charged to replicate would be something that picked up these thematic
elements, whether it was a river environment, where
we all floated down rafts, crawling with crocodile and
hundreds of hippos outside of our rowboats. The types

of plants nearby, whether they're African baobab trees or all the different species, growing down to these rivers and environments with seasonal rains to produce fruit and wood and timber.

We had specific images and within the confines of the space we were allowed, working with the amount of time you'd have for, say, the African safari, we would try to get in a forest and a hippo river, then a wooded higher headland before rolling out to the wooded grasslands.

Comstock combed the Earth for years on end to acquire seeds, plants, and shrubs, and not just for their aesthetic qualities. The park designers realized, as Comstock put it so aptly, that Animal Kingdom was the first theme park "where the actors eat the scenery." During his travels to 37 states in America and 28 countries around the globe, he literally stuffed millions of seeds into plastic bags and jammed those bags into his luggage, all so that they could be propagated and replanted in Florida to feed and nourish members of the park's always-hungry "cast." Perhaps more importantly, the wide variety of trees and plants that were acquired needed to be planted years in advance of the park's opening, allowing them time to mature. The end result: when Animal Kingdom opened, the foliage looked as if it had been on the property for years, if not decades.

A little more than a year after the Animal Kingdom project started, it was abruptly put on hold. Several factors came into the decision to go on hiatus, not the least of which was the emphasis on getting Euro Disneyland (now Disneyland Paris) in Marne-la-Vallee, France, open on time. With the Animal Kingdom project on hold, some members of the Animal Kingdom design team were reassigned to Euro Disneyland.

Paul Comstock took his botanical expertise to France, where he worked on the foliage in the Frontierland section of that park. The experience proved to be quite educational and he was able to transfer that newly acquired information to Animal Kingdom when work resumed about a year later.

According to Comstock, with the project on hold:

> My department manager said, "Well, if Paul isn't going to be designing and building something here, we're

going to send him to Paris to work on Euro Disneyland."
My first assignment there was to rebuild the forest in
Frontierland. When I looked at the plans, all the trees
were in neat rows. My first task was to try to deconstruct
that and make it look more natural. But to make it so
that three trees don't line up in a straight line is really
a hard thing to do. Actually, the exercise of doing that
in Paris, bringing back that knowledge, kind of helped in
furthering this idea to our team, that when we re-create
Africa or part of Asia, these areas aren't laid out. The idea
really was to create a type of a landscape that was very
fertile, where the colors and the contrast of the materials
were very harlequin-type patterns—not straight rows or
very clean-looking, like throughout Epcot Center. When
you stay and live in a rain forest and you see this incredible diversity and the struggle for light to shine through
when you have this forested canopy, [you learn how to
replicate] this incredible landscape.

During the hiatus, Mickey Steinberg, Sklar's right-hand
man at Imagineering, convinced management to keep most
of Animal Kingdom's core design team intact, thus allowing
them to continue working on the project, specifically on
drawing packages for various elements of the park, until work
resumed. "The influence this had on contractors' bids, and the
schedule, was enormously positive," Sklar said.

In addition, Comstock and Evans convinced Disney's higher-ups to continue their plant propagation program during
the break.

Sklar said:

Paul and Bill came to us and said, "If we don't get out
ahead of what's going on in the southeast United States,
we're going to lose a lot of the specimens we're going to
need for the project." We were able to give them a budget
of $3 million up front when the project was on hiatus,
so they could go out and collect the kind of materials
they needed. I remember it was particularly important
that Bill and Paul get those bamboo trees that they had
made in Georgia.

The bamboo trees, which grow quickly to more than 40 feet tall, were important to the park's landscape as they provided food for some of the animals, as well as fulfilling shade, habitat, and scenery needs. The bamboos also supplied a natural wind-break barrier for the park.

No sooner had work on the park picked up again when the project seemed to teeter on the brink once more. In 1994, a series of events sent shockwaves throughout the company and forced some within the Disney hierarchy to rethink Animal Kingdom. First, Disney president Frank Wells, Eisner's right-hand man and one of the park's biggest proponents, died in a helicopter crash on April 3. Then, in July, Eisner suffered a heart attack which required open-heart surgery. When Jeffrey Katzenberg, head of Disney Animation, wasn't given Wells' job, he abruptly left the company. To top it off, an Eisner-inspired theme park project in Virginia, called Disney's America, fell flat on its face as the result of stiff community opposition. The 1990s, which Eisner had dubbed "the Disney decade," were in jeopardy of becoming a Disney dud. In the face of all this, and with some in his inner circle advising him to pull the plug on Animal Kingdom, Eisner—as he had been since the beginning of the project—remained firm in his commitment to the park, saying:

> Standing still is not an option. Either you take calculated risks to grow, or you slowly wither and die.

With a renewed sense of commitment, Disney and the Animal Kingdom design team soldiered on.

Among the myriad design challenges faced by the team: an icon for the new park. The Magic Kingdom has its Cinderella Castle, Epcot has Spaceship Earth, and Hollywood Studios has alternated between Earffel Tower and Sorcerer Mickey's hat. What type of structure would best embody Animal Kingdom, its mission, and everything it stands for, from a conservation standpoint?

After much debate, the designers settled on a tree. A Tree of Life, to be specific, a massive structure that stands 145 feet tall (the use of forced perspective, so prevalent in the Magic Kingdom, was not necessary here). The tree reflects Animal Kingdom's true message: how the Earth's animal population is all intertwined, all connected, all reliant on one another, all in need of care and respect. Carved into the massive trunk and roots are the heads of 325 animals, most representing animals still walking the planet today, others either mythical or extinct. In the area surrounding the tree trunk are small pools and meadows, which a collection of birds, mammals, and reptiles calls home.

Keeping in mind that this "tree" is, in reality, a building, one that had to be able to withstand hurricane-force winds, Disney's planners employed design techniques typically used for offshore oil rigs. They even incorporated expansion joints, which connect each branch to the trunk.

Rohde explained:

> The Tree of Life is a technological marvel, but it's a symbol of the beauty and diversity and the grandeur of animal life on Earth. It's a celebration of our emotions about animals and their habitat.

Rick Barongi tells a great story of how one animal was added to the tree's "collection" very late in the process, at the insistence of one of the world's preeminent animal experts:

> I knew Jane Goodall very well and I invited her out to the Tree of Life site when it was under construction. Just the two of us were walking around the park late in the afternoon. The scaffolding was up about 100 feet on the tree and I took her up there, which I wasn't supposed to do and I got in trouble for it, but it was Jane Goodall, so they left me alone. We're looking at these hundreds of animals carved into the tree and she says, "This is wonderful, Rick, this is amazing...but there's no chimp." I said, "Oh, there's got to be a chimp." And she said, "I've been looking and there's no chimp."
>
> I go back the next day and I approach Joe and his assistant Jennifer [Gerstin, who, along with Joe Rohde, are among just a few Animal Kingdom originals still working at Imagineering] and I say, "Hey guys, Jane Goodall says there's no chimp on the tree," and I asked them if there was still time to put one in. And Joe says I should talk to Zsolt [Hormay, the tree's lead sculptor]. I met Zsolt at

my site and I asked him if he could put another animal on the tree. And he said, "Sure, which one?" "We need a chimp." He asked me to send him a picture.

I sent him a picture of David Greybeard, Jane's favorite chimp. I didn't hear from Zsolt for about a month. Then, I called him up and he said, "Come out tomorrow and I'll show you." I show up the next day and at the entrance to the theater, at the base of the tree, is this huge figure of David Greybeard, bigger than life, with his hand stretched out. We ended up doing a plaque, dedicating it to Jane Goodall. The day we opened, Michael Eisner presented it to her and it just blew her away. That story, to me, is incredible...there's one animal on that Tree of Life that's based on a real animal. It was all because of Zsolt Hormay. I made sure Jane got to meet Zsolt that day.

On the morning of April 21, 1998, the park was dedicated prior to an all-day media-only event. A number of Disney dignitaries and show-business celebrities were on hand for the all-day press bash, in keeping with Disney's tradition of making park openings one-of-a-kind *events*. Drew Carey, then the star of *The Drew Carey Show* and the host of a television special on Animal Kingdom's opening, showed up dressed in a faux leopard suit, taking poor taste to new depths. Actress Kathy Kinney, Carey's nemesis on the show, also was on hand for the festivities, as were Michael J. Fox, Leonardo DiCaprio, and *Home Improvement*'s Richard Karn. Some of the big news of the day included Frank Sinatra being released from the hospital after what was described as a routine checkup (he would die three weeks later), and a grieving Paul McCartney paying tribute to his wife, Linda, who passed away four days before.

The following day, April 22—appropriately, Earth Day—Disney's Animal Kingdom swung open its gates to the public, accompanied by much anticipation and fanfare. Ticket prices were $44.52 for adults and $36.04 for children 3–9. They all came to see this new species of theme park on the day it was born. But like any living thing in its infancy, the park was a bit wobbly on its feet and needed time to grow and mature.

CHAPTER THREE

Plants and Animals

When the phrase "job interview" is mentioned, it usually conjures images of sweaty palms, intimidating interviewers, and plenty of angst on the part of the interviewee.

Paul Comstock had already been working for Walt Disney Imagineering for several months when he experienced perhaps the world's quickest and easiest job interview:

> I was working on a couple things [at Disneyland] when I got a phone call. It was Joe [Rohde], saying, "We're out in one of the funky trailers in the parking lot and we have an idea for an attraction and we need a landscape architect. Can you come over?" I said, "Sure, I'll be there." I sat in at one meeting and afterwards Joe basically said, "Would you like to be on this team? We want to build a landscape and put animals in it." I started that way.

It turns out Paul Comstock had been training most of his life to be Animal Kingdom's principal landscape architect:

> My interest in landscaping goes back pretty far, to my grandmother. When I was a kid growing up, my grandmother lived in Corona del Mar, down by the beach, and I would spend a lot of time with her. And my father was a plantsman. I guess it kind of really started when I was growing up. I come from a large family, eight children, and just about every time we moved into a larger house, my father would build a new garden. So, at an early age, I kind of learned all the basics, from preparing the soil, which is the main thing with all gardens, to planting grass, to shrubs and planting trees of all different sizes.
>
> When it came time in my life to earn some money of my own, I had volunteered to do something for a friend,

digging irrigation ditches and trenches for a project near the Rose Bowl on one of these really beautiful homes on Architects' Row. The owner said to me, "What would you do?" I said I would get a few big boulders here and put something else there...and that turned into a landscape that won several awards. It was just all really built on what I had absorbed growing up and working with my dad, putting some large boulders here and planting some trees here to anchor bases, basically building something that had a thematic thread. So that led me to building waterfalls and designing landscapes throughout southern California.

Comstock worked for his father's company, Monrovia Nursery, the largest container nursery in the world. Every fall, Monrovia participated in a fall garden show in Los Angeles and one year, Comstock's dad encouraged him to build something for the show:

I designed a little garden space with a waterfall, a little gazebo area and a little path. A cute little garden space. [At one point during the show] Bill Evans, who was a Disneyland original, walked up to me and literally tapped me on the shoulder, introduced himself, and said in a raspy voice, "How would you like to do a really large landscape?" And I said, "Sure!"

With Evans' help, Comstock enrolled in a program at UCLA which pointed him in the direction of becoming a licensed landscaping architect:

I was installing and designing landscapes during the day and going to school at night. [Two years into that four-year program, I got a call from Evans, who said,] "Why don't you come over and show me what you're doing?"

I showed him some stuff and he said, "OK, I want you to go work for the guy [Joe Linesch] who is the director of landscaping for WED, before it became Imagineering. Joe basically did the design for Epcot and did a number of other projects at Disneyland. After I worked for Joe for almost three years, Bill said I should now come to work for Disney. My hire date was Feb. 5, 1990. They interviewed me in 1989. I bought my first suit for the interview. I wore it for the first few days after I was hired and one of the other landscape architects who had been there for 15 years said, "Paul, I really like you, but do me a favor and stop wearing that suit!"

After agreeing to join Animal Kingdom's design team, Comstock and his cohorts had to figure out just what to put on the "unremarkable" land where Animal Kingdom was to be built. It was, to paraphrase Marty Sklar, the ultimate blank sheet of paper. While the other members of the team tossed around dozens of concepts for attractions within the park, it was Comstock's responsibility to design the landscaping that would support each one of those ideas. Moreover, those landscapes would have to mirror those that you'd typically find in different parts of the world, such as a savannah in Africa or a jungle in Asia.

Perhaps most importantly, those flourishing landscapes, filled with myriad trees, plants, and grasses, had to be animal friendly. The team learned a crucial lesson early on when it came to how critical the plant-animal relationship is.

According to Comstock, it all began with the selection of a site for the park:

> There were a couple of options on the table for corporate. One of them was a piece of property that is south of Osceola Parkway, which is now the city of Celebration. They sent us out there to look at the Celebration property as well as the site where Animal Kingdom is now. And what we were visualizing was a lot of elevation change, so we needed a large, contiguous space. I remember being totally enamored with the huge oaks that were on the Celebration site, but it really had some dewatering problems, in terms of the amount of water that was on the site that would come to the surface of the ground. They ultimately made it into a big lake.
>
> We knew at that time that we needed a site that was high and dry for the health of the livestock. Actually, in developing this kind of fun, dreamy idea, we had to learn a lot about animal husbandry, what keeps animals healthy

and what can be detrimental to them. On the landscape side, we had to figure out what was toxic. If we had this beautiful plant on the property that looked really great from the point of view of a scene, but it was toxic to an animal, we had to make sure they weren't included. An example of that: the Animal Kingdom site is bordered on both sides by Reedy Creek and Boggy Creek. On the area where we wanted to put the black rhinoceros, which are very rare, we learned that literally five leaves from a native maple tree that grows near Boggy Creek could potentially kill a full-grown black rhinoceros.

The team enlisted the help of "some great animal experts from Seattle" and they combined to create an environment that was both beautiful and non-threatening to the permanent residents of the park.

When the team first drove over what would become the Animal Kingdom site, Comstock knew they had hit pay dirt:

We drove over the cow pasture in a four-wheel-drive Suburban and got stuck in pure white Florida sugar sand. I said, "This land will support a park. If we can sterilize the native plants so we have a clean palette, we'll be able to grow anything we want to in here." The dry sand means there's drainage, which is the key to building any landscape. If you think of hydroponics, plants can grow in mid-air if you can nourish the roots with nutrients. Dirt and sand are just an armature so that the plant can stand upright. So, by being on land that's high enough on the water table, I went, "Oh man, we found it!"

In addition, the site selected had the proper sun orientation, which is one of those little-known, yet key design elements for siting a Disney park:

The Celebration site was facing the wrong way. When you'd be driving on the Osceola Parkway, you'd be driving into the sunlight. The way that Animal Kingdom is oriented, you enter and the sun arc is behind your back, so it illuminates the park...the trees, the structures, the Tree of Life, all the waterfalls, all those things are positioned in the right way for the sun arc. If you look at all the other

Disney parks, except for Hong Kong, they're all positioned where the light shines on the castle as you walk
down Main Street. The sun rises in the east and either
goes behind you or overhead. It's never in total shadow so
that you always have that perfect Kodak moment.

In addition to creating an aesthetically pleasing landscape, Comstock was charged with bringing back seeds
and plants from around the world that would help feed the
animals. To that end, Joe Rohde was, as Comstock put it, "our
guardian angel":

> Joe first took us to the older world, to Africa and Asia,
> to see these places, to kind of dip our brains into that
> environment, so that we could smell it and see it and feel
> it. Total immersion in the real thing.

Then, as the team quickly learned, there had to be a distinction between what looked good from the guests' perspective
and what was safe and beneficial to the animals. Every plant
has a different level of toxicity. Learning what plants might be
harmful to certain animals was a challenge:

> The very first kind of filter was, "What would be the
> kind of plants from the areas themselves that we could
> collect, bring back, and grow that weren't toxic, not be
> on the invasive species list, and not have any potential
> issues that anybody could call us on.

During the team's travels, Comstock learned another
valuable lesson:

> All of the Disney parks, starting with Disneyland and
> including the parks in Florida and all of our parks glob-
> ally, are considered national botanic gardens. There are
> global rules that botanical gardens have in their charters
> which allow the transmission of plant materials—seed
> and living tissue, in the forms of cuttings, and there
> are size restrictions for actual plants. There are inter-
> national laws which the United States is party to that
> allows for the transmission of these materials. Seeds,
> cuttings, seedlings, what have you. We did our home-
> work as a team and made sure everything that we were
> going after was 100% within all legal jurisdictions.

There's an organization called CITES [Congress on International Trade in Endangered Species]. It's a global organization that puts plant materials into several different categories: ones that are threatened, ones that cannot be moved, ones that are endemic to a certain area. Any movement of them in and out of botanical gardens is governed by this organization. We did our homework and made sure that everything that we were going after thematically met these standards and supported the concept art and leadership direction by Joe Rohde of what he wanted these spaces to look like.

Although Comstock was famous for stuffing seeds into plastic bags and jamming them into his suitcases, he was extra careful to make sure everything he did was on the up and up:

What I would do was to get all the legal things done for the shipment. If I was importing seed from India or Nepal or Thailand or South Africa, we would go through all the legal channels with the USDA [United States Department of Agriculture]. We would tell them that we were going after these seeds or going after these plants. A lot of them are produced for international shipping, and a lot of these companies...there are people who you can contact and say, "I want to buy 200 of this type of tree." It's all above board and they send it to you in the mail.

The idea of growing the animals' food either on property or in nearby nurseries proved both practical and cost-effective. Comstock worked closely with Dennis Higbie, Animal Kingdom's general curator of botanical programs, in the years leading up to the park's opening. Over the years, Disney's horticulture team has been largely responsible for growing the plants needed to feed—and amuse—the animals. Its massive backstage greenhouse "is dedicated largely to growing vegetables, grasses, and other nutritious plants" for Animal Kingdom's residents, said Doug Benedict of the horticulture team, adding:

Some of the animals consume so many crops that we don't plant them in their habitats. We drop them into sleeves hidden in the ground, the animals graze, and we replace them with a fresh batch.

The horticulturalists also will place large tree limbs on the savannah so elephants can push them around for the fun of it or they'll put palm trees in the gorillas' enclosure so the large primates can amuse themselves or assert their dominance by ripping them down. Among the other food items on the "menu" are mulberry, bananas, herbs, and a popular soft vegetation called browse. Indeed, the keepers at the park go through about 3,000 pounds of cut browse every day.

In addition to the food aspect of Animal Kingdom's foliage, it was quickly surmised that landscaping would be the dominant aspect of the park and would be an essential part of its story (as opposed to the other Disney parks, where landscaping is used an enhancement). As such, there needed to be a set of ground rules. Insecticides and other pest-control chemicals, particularly those in pellet form (which could be mistaken as seeds by animals) could not be used. Every decision made had to take into consideration animal welfare, plant health, and environmental impact. Finally, man-made areas such as the savannah needed to look natural, not neat and manicured, like the landscaping in Epcot. As Higbie put it, "There was so much we had to unlearn."

The fertilizer products used at Disney's Animal Kingdom, according to Higbie, were approved by select animal programs' veterinary staff and nutrition groups and were determined to be harmless to animals. It was one of countless measures taken by Disney to ensure the safety and well-being of all the animals who would be living on the property

While much study and thought was given to the plant life on Animal Kingdom's 500-plus acres, caring for the more than 1,000 animals on property was clearly Job One. To that end, some of the country's leading animal-care specialists were recruited to assist in setting up the elaborate system that would care, feed, and nurture the permanent residents of the park.

Leading that initiative was Rick Barongi, who came to Disney as a well-respected member of the country's conservationist and animal-care community and a veteran of several major zoos in America.

Like Joe Rohde, Rick Barongi brought an extensive resume of international travel to the Animal Kingdom project. He was born in the New York City borough of Queens and was raised on Long Island. As a child, he had a typical collection of pets—dogs, hamsters, turtles. But then he paid a visit to the Natural History Museum in Manhattan, where he saw the gorilla figure on display. At that moment, his life's path seemed to be charted for him. Right after college, Barongi traveled to Africa in 1974, a trip he described as life-altering:

> That first trip to Africa when I was 21 years old, right out of college, changed my life more than any one experience. It was only four months, because that's all that my money lasted. I didn't know anybody. I had some letters of introduction and I met some really interesting people over there, [including Joy Adamson of *Born Free* fame during the filming of that TV show in Kenya].

Adamson provided Barongi with a letter of recommendation to see Dr. Paul Sayer, head veterinarian at the University of Nairobi. He tried, but failed, to meet with gorilla researcher Dian Fossey, but he did manage to visit with her stunning collection of gorillas. Another highlight of his Africa adventure came when he traveled to the Republic of Congo, where he saw a variety of African animals in their natural habitats. Before his tenure with Disney, Barongi made more than 20 return trips to Africa, as well as visiting animal refuges in Australia, New Zealand, South America, and Russia. He even went to Panama to help rescue the private animal collection of General Manuel Noriega after the deposed dictator abandoned them.

Of his African travels, Barongi said:

> You go to Africa for any length of time, it usually changes you. Not as a tourist, but living there the way I did, traveling through the country, backpacking for a month to see gorillas. You're on buses and trains in these little villages. I think that really impacted my life. On the animal side, it gave me a much greater perspective on things, understanding the bigger picture. I take a lot of people to Africa now, mostly because they become more engaged and they're more likely to support conservation.

Barongi began as a consultant on the Animal Kingdom project, but was eventually hired full-time as the director of

Animal Project Development. His first task was to recruit some of the best animal-care experts from the country's leading zoos, many of whom he had worked with:

> We didn't announce the park publicly until 1995. Marty Sklar and Joe Rohde let me bring in outside people. And Judson Green [president of Walt Disney Attractions at the time] was very important. Those three really put a lot of faith in this young guy...me. They said they wanted me to establish a program of care and conservation *before* we opened the park and not *after*.

Barongi faced a three-pronged challenge: hire respected animal caregivers, acquire more than 1,000 animals for those caregivers to work with, and assist in the design of the savannah, where many of the animals would call home. Although the animals were—and still are—the top priority, creating a pleasant work environment for the animal caregivers also was important, especially to Barongi:

> I think the other thing that helped was the facilities where the animals stayed at night. We upped that level of sophistication [for the keepers who tend to the animals overnight]. Most of the buildings had staff break rooms, computers, and bathrooms. This allowed the keepers to stay with the animals. They didn't have to walk across the property to use the bathrooms. That's a little thing, but I remember architects who walked around and looked at the facilities and said, "Wow, we're really impressed with this. No zoo has a backhouse like this.

Among Barongi's many noteworthy hires was Dr. Peregrine Wolff, Animal Kingdom's director of Veterinary Services on opening day. After earning degrees in animal sciences from the University of Vermont and veterinary medicine from Cornell University, she gained valuable experience at the Lincoln Park Zoo in Chicago and the Minnesota Zoo near Minneapolis. She came to Animal Kingdom with a wealth of knowledge, experience and enthusiasm.

Wolff said:

> What's exciting about the programs at Disney's Animal Kingdom is that many different animals live in very

natural habitats. Years ago, many zoos had very poor sanitation practices, then they got too sterile, making the animals' environment barren, without the complexity that animals require for good health.

She oversaw a staff of four veterinarians. In addition to the veterinary care facilities, Animal Kingdom has a quarantine station, where incoming animals need to be tested up to 90 days for diseases and parasites before they can be released into the general population.

Barongi also had a hand in bringing many of the country's leading animal experts on board, with each possessing a unique skill set. They included Dr. Beth Stevens, Director of Conservation and Science; Bruce Read, General Curator; Joe Christman, Curator of Large Mammals; John Lehnhardt, Elephant Curator; Dr. Nancy Pratt, Curator of Primates and Small Mammals; Connie Philipp, Zoological Manager of Gorillas; Grenville Roles, Curator of Birds; Dr. Jill Mellen; Research Biologist; Marty Sevenich, Curator of Behavioral Husbandry; Dr. Jackie Ogden, Curator of Conservation Station; and Kathryn Lehnhardt, Curator of Education and Guest Experiences.

With a talented team on board, Barongi went about the seemingly impossible task of getting animals of every shape and size to central Florida:

> Acquiring more than 1,000 animals was a big project, and it was a big part of my job. When I started, I was the only full-time employee; the rest were advisors working on the project part-time. We had to put a list together of the animals we needed. I got to pick most of the animals for the safari. You had to base it on things like the climate and the holding areas. I always said Joe Rohde wanted a lot more animals, but the landscape wouldn't tolerate it. It would be a dust bowl out there, even if you put them away at night. You could still have a lot of animals, but you had to be smart about it. Paul Comstock was designing a smorgasbord out there, like a buffet. He just said, "We'll put it all out there. After they eat it, we'll put more out there." He's as passionate about plants as I am about animals. He's a great guy, a brilliant guy.

I put a lot of work into animal acquisition. Most of these animals were in breeding programs where the AZA [Association of Zoos and Aquariums] was involved and there were plenty of animals out there to have. The only challenge on availability were the elephants and gorillas. Elephants were a very challenging acquisition. We were going to get them out of the wild because they were culling them and they were going to die if we didn't take them, but then there was a moratorium on culling. With the gorillas, we wanted a family group. There were about 20 zoos in front of us waiting for female gorillas. We thought we'd do two groups of exhibits, a bachelor group and a family group. I told the gorilla planning group that I was going to look for the gorillas myself, that we couldn't wait in line. It sounds arrogant, but I knew that on opening day, we needed a family of gorillas out there.

I worked directly with the Lincoln Park Zoo, because I knew they had enough gorillas that they could give us a whole family. We worked out a deal with them. You don't buy the gorillas, you don't pay for them. Instead, we offered to form a gorilla conservation fund with them and sponsor a project and that's what we did in return for the gorillas. The other zoos were mad at that because they said now we were offering money for gorillas. In a sense, they were right, but my question was, "Why didn't you do the same thing, give more money for gorilla conservation?"

The acquisition of the gorilla family gave Animal Kingdom one of its first "stars": Gino.

That was a big acquisition and they gave us a great group of gorillas. Gino, the male, was in that family and he's still there. A family of gorillas touches you in ways that other animals don't, especially their social skills. When there's a baby born, they protect it. Gino was born in the Rotterdam Zoo and was bottle raised. Then he came to the Lincoln Park Zoo, so he's been around people all his life. He was great with the other gorillas and the babies. We had a lot of silverbacks, but he was the only true silverback.

Gino and the other gorillas (a gorilla's lifespan is typically 35–40 years) can be seen living in the lap of luxury—at least for gorillas—along the Gorilla Falls Exploration Trail in the Africa section of the park.

Comstock and Barongi joined forces to help create the savannah, which would be the setting for Kilimanjaro Safaris. Comstock put his wealth of knowledge to work in crafting a lush green forest, complemented by rivers and waterfalls, as well as a replica of the Serengeti grasslands. On that sweeping landscape, Barongi would place a potpourri of wildlife, everything from antelope, okapis, giraffes, zebras, rhinos, elephants, crocodiles, lions, hippos, ostriches, and others. The challenge was to make it seem as natural as if the safari vehicles were motoring through a savannah in Africa...and as comfortable to those creatures who would inhabit the land.

Barongi said:

> On the design of the savannah, I had to be deeply involved because I didn't have an animal staff at the time. What I'd do was bring in some of my colleagues for a day or two of planning. I'd say, "Hey, I'm sitting here with Disney and these Imagineers, and whatever I tell them, they believe. They do exactly what I say because they don't know anything about animals. I need you guys to come in and play devil's advocate with them because I know I'm not always going to be doing the best thing." They need to hear this debate. So, I purposely brought people in as consultants.

Members of Jones & Jones Architects were contracted to design the animal habitats. The lead landscape architect, Duane Dietz, designed the animal enclosures and exhibits visible to guests in Africa, DinoLand U.S.A., and near the Tree of Life. Pat Janikowski designed the animal holding buildings, while Jim Brighton was chiefly responsible for the gorilla enclosure, the Pangani Forest Exploration Trail (now the Gorilla Falls Exploration Trail), and the animal areas in Asia. (Janikowski and Brighton currently are partners in the Seattle zoo architectural firm PJA Architects.)

Barongi said:

They worked very closely with me, and deserve as much credit as anybody, because they were zoo architects and because they knew the landscaping. And then you'd have Paul Comstock, who marched to his own drummer. He's putting stuff out there all over the place. We did wire some trees because I told him that the giraffes are going to decimate everything if you don't protect the trees. It was a group process when you don't have a staff.

And when the staff did get hired a year later, they looked and me and said, "Why did you do that this way? Why didn't we get more of this?" They didn't understand the process. Also, no matter how much money we had—and we had a lot—I was always being pressured to "value engineer." I hate that term now, but there were people on the construction side who made it sound like we couldn't finish the job, that we were running out of money, but I knew we had plenty of money. I would try to cut things to make it look good. Joe would defend me and Marty Sklar would really defend me on that and so would Judson Green; he was the key to the whole thing as well. All these operations at Imagineering have this friction when they design the park and they'd hand it over to the operators and the operators would try to do something that would violate the concept or the storyline and they'd go back and forth. In the end, it all worked.

When Animal Kingdom swung open its gates on April 22, 1998, guests were amazed by the wide assortment of animals within view, seemingly at every turn; the lush, full-grown landscape; and the not-so-subtle messages of conservation and preservation. Although nearly 20 years have passed since the park opened, the level of care among Animal Kingdom's staff to both animal and plant life has remained consistently high.

Dr. Scott Terrell, who is now the director of Animal and Scientific Operations for Disney, has been on staff at Animal Kingdom since 1997. He's an expert on every animal on the property and exhibits an incredible level of compassion and commitment, very much like the rest of the park's behind-the-scenes animal care staff.

When he was asked about the most high-maintenance animal among Animal Kingdom's 1,000-plus creatures, Dr. Terrell was quick to respond:

> Zebras. They require a lot of attention, especially their hoofs. They're basically horses, so we have to make sure their hoofs are really pristine, so they get a lot of attention. In order to work with them, we have to anesthetize them. They take a lot of work.

So, too, Terrell added, do the park's precious rhinos:

> Because rhinos are so critically endangered, especially our black rhinos, they receive the utmost care. We're not in a breeding situation right now, but we pay a lot of attention to our female, particularly if she were to breed someday. There are so few left, maybe 5,000 black rhinos and 20,000 white rhinos left in the world. The poachers have almost decimated their populations, all for the horns. A typical horn can fetch about $80,000 U.S., on the black market, so that's several years' income for a lot of people. There was a tragedy in Paris several months ago where several criminals broke into a zoo and took the rhino. There have been incidents where people have broken into museums and stolen horns. We have pretty good security here, though.

Indeed, Terrell said, Animal Kingdom, all 500-plus acres, is the ultimate gated community:

> The entire park is fenced in, in large part to keep predators, both animal and human, from getting in. We also have cameras on all the fences.

According to Terrell, staffers who work with the permanent residents of Animal Kingdom must be on their toes at all times:

> There's always something new going on. We have a little social issue with our crocs right now. They're all boys. We have 23 boys, and boys will be boys. They're always fighting. They actually have features so they can be self-identified. When they came to us they were all about four feet long, now they measure up to 11 feet long and weigh about 750 pounds. They're trained to

shift backstage as well and we have an area that they voluntarily go in to so we can treat them. We have a CAT scan that's big enough that they can fit in it. They get as good care as we get, sometimes better.

Indeed, the animals on property receive regular medical attention. It's not unusual for them to be taken to the care facilities in Rafiki's Planet Watch to receive inoculations, treatment for injuries, or dental work. In addition, the animals receive a diet rich in nutrients. "We're sort of the world's leading facility when it comes to nutrition for the animals," Terrell said.

Bruce Read, who was general curator when Animal Kingdom opened, explained:

Feeding animals is a science. Diet is an important part of their daily care. With so many different animals on property, diet also has to be varied...often wildly so. An elephant, for instance, eats 125 pounds of food per day, mostly a hay and pelleted energy-based ration. Anteaters, as you might expect, eat ants, but they also consume a diet rich in grubs. Birds are a whole other world. They eat across the whole spectrum. Some eat rodents, some eat seeds. They're a real challenge.

Diversity is an important part of the feeding process. We change their diets, but not to the point that it upsets their stomachs. We get the same quality produce that people get at their grocery stores.

Several birds flew overhead as Terrell continued to talk about Animal Kingdom:

Those are our macaws. They're free-flight and occasionally they go on "vacation," but most of the time they do come back and they get a reward when they return. That's really the way zoos should be going, where animals display natural behaviors.

Marty Sklar pointed out that breeding is a welcomed byproduct of caring for the animals in the park:

The births of so many animals that are on the property over the years is really exciting. I think we started with about 1,000 animals. I don't know how many are there now, but I do know the animals are at home there. They really feel as if they're in a place that they should be.

On breeding, Terrell explained:

Tigers can be very difficult to breed. If a male and a female don't get along, they've been known to fight with one another, sometimes to the death. Fortunately, our male and female tigers are on pretty good terms.

We recently had a baby elephant born here. Stella is up to 600 pounds, but she can't quite feed herself yet. She actually won't feed herself for about two years because she's practicing using her trunk. She'll be on Mom's milk until she's about 5, but she's always practicing how to use her trunk. She was about 240 pounds when she was born on Dec. 14, 2016. She's been a pistol.

(Stella's mother, Donna, had given birth to two other calves, Nadira and Luna, before Stella came into the world.)

And we just had 40 baby otters born on Discovery Island. Their big thing is to learn how to swim. The moms love water, but the dads don't, so every time the moms put the babies in the water, the dads pull them out. Otters don't know how to swim; they have to be taught by their parents.

Terrell said that pandas, a mainstay at many zoos around the world, will likely never be seen at Animal Kingdom:

We haven't talked seriously about pandas here. Really the heart and soul of Disney's Animal Kingdom is you have the animals and you have the story. Right now, the story of pandas wouldn't really fit into the story of the park. We're very India, Southeast Asia, and Africa-based, so pandas aren't in our long-term plans.

And pandas come with a lot of baggage, politically. They're also not the most exciting animals, either. They kind of just sit around. They do make money for zoos that have them, but that income has to be shared, that's part of the deal.

In addition to his work at Animal Kingdom, Dr. Terrell supervises animal care at other Disney parks, including Disneyland Paris, where horses, cattle and buffalo are part of the Buffalo Bill's Wild West Show. He's also an advocate for animals:

> We're trying to reverse the trend when it comes to species dying off. Incredible things are happening, like the butterflies at Disney's Vero Beach Resort. There was a species there that was almost extinct, but now they're back. That's our focus now.

CHAPTER FOUR

Opening Day

It's a tradition that was born on a steamy July afternoon in 1955, when Walt Disney read from a plaque as he dedicated Disneyland in Anaheim, California. Over the years, every time a new Disney park has opened (there are 12 of them worldwide), the chairman of the company at the time has followed in Walt's footsteps, reading from a plaque during formal dedication ceremonies. On April 21, 1998, then-Disney CEO and chairman Michael Eisner did the honors for Animal Kingdom:

> Welcome to a kingdom of animals...real, ancient and imagined; A kingdom ruled by lions, dinosaurs and dragons; a kingdom of balance, harmony and survival; a kingdom we enter to share in the wonder, gaze at the beauty, thrill at the drama...and learn.

Eisner told those gathered at the park's entrance:

> Nature is perhaps the greatest storyteller of all. From the smallest ant to the biggest bull elephant, the true-life stories of animals are fascinating and ever changing—indeed, that's the one aspect that sets the Animal Kingdom apart.

He went on to honor the park's advisory board, a team of naturalists, environmentalists, and zoologists who had worked behind the scenes to ensure that Animal Kingdom met the highest standards of animal care and environmental awareness, and then praised park consultant Jane Goodall, recognized around the world for her work with chimpanzees in the wild.

Eisner added:

> In a way, the Animal Kingdom takes us full circle. Thirty years ago, all of you could find on our Orlando property were vast herds of grazing animals and some rather

intimidating reptiles. Today, after billions of dollars in investment, we have unveiled our most original theme park concept yet: Vast herds of grazing animals and some rather intimidating reptiles.

Roy E. Disney, Walt's nephew, also was on hand for the festivities, which was fitting, since it was Roy E. who kickstarted his own Disney career by producing and co-directing many of the True-Life Adventures films and who is credited with getting the ball rolling on the creation of an animal-themed park.

Roy said:

> Just as this theme park has its roots in our films, it also represents a major departure. Once a movie is completed, it's done forever. On the other hand, Disney's Animal Kingdom—like the animal world itself—will evolve and grow. It's truly a living thing...something we are consciously and proudly calling "Disney's."

On opening day, Animal Kingdom comprised more than 500 acres. There were approximately 2,500 cast members employed at the park. A massive parking lot could accommodate 6,000 cars outside, while inside, about 1,000 animals, representing 200 species—most acquired from zoos accredited by the Association of Zoos and Aquariums, some rare and endangered—had been living on the property for months. From a landscaping perspective, four million trees, plants, shrubs, grasses, ferns, and vines, representing 3,000 species, were flourishing when those first guests made their way into the park. Outside the park, a system of new roads handled the anticipated influx of motor vehicles on opening day and beyond.

A Florida Department of Transportation spokesman said of Disney's proactive approach:

> There are additional access points that didn't exist previously. They haven't contacted us to tell us they anticipate any particular problems.

A spokesman for the Florida Highway Patrol added:

> Another theme park is certainly an added burden with the traffic. It's going to be our job to keep the roads clear as quick as we can.

Attendance on opening day—and, indeed, over the next several months—far exceeded projections, so those new roads were quickly put to the test.

Eisner said:

> Whatever doubts we may once have had about the Animal Kingdom's viability were answered on the day the park opened. The crowds were so large that we were forced to close our gates to further guests by 9 a.m. Over the next few months, attendance has exceeded every expectation, and the ratings from guests are the highest we've received for any park in our history.

Park brochures welcomed guests to:

> Disney's wildest adventure yet, [a place where] the fun and excitement of a Disney theme park is mixed with the thrill of adventure in the wild. Every path and trail leads to fun, thrills and adventure with the real, imaginary and extinct creatures who rule this kingdom. It's the imagination of Disney, gone wild!

The new park was divided into seven themed areas: the Oasis, Safari Village, Camp Minnie-Mickey, Africa, Conservation Station, Asia, and DinoLand U.S.A. Although Asia was listed as a "land," it was still under construction and consisted of just one attraction, Flights of Wonder, on opening day. At several of the park's attractions—Countdown to Extinction, It's Tough to Be a Bug, Festival of the Lion King, Pangani Forest Exploration Trail (now the Gorilla Falls Exploration Trail), and Kilimanjaro Safaris—cast members handed out limited-edition pins to appreciative guests, each pin themed to that particular attraction; as you might expect, the pins became instant collectors' items.

Upon entering the park, guests noticed that the cast members at Animal Kingdom were wearing clothing that was as diverse as the animals in the park: Costumes needed to reflect the jobs each cast member performed, from bright native clothing for Harambe's cast members to safari wear to animal care givers' costumes to the animal figure designs worn by the cast in Safari Village. In all, there were 62 different designs worn by Animal Kingdom cast members scattered throughout the park. On opening day, 20 percent of the cast costumes were made of lyocell, a natural, environmentally friendly fabric made from wood pulp.

Patty Dunne, the coordinator of costume design for the park, said:

> Because there's limited climate control in the park, this new technology is one of many cutting-edge ideas that are most helpful in meeting demands for comfort, durability, and authentic looks.

As with the opening of most of the other Disney parks, a hardy group of people camped outside the gate the night before in hopes of becoming the first guests to enter. The honor of being the first family to walk through Animal Kingdom's turnstiles fell to Brenda Herr of St. Petersburg, Florida; her husband, Damon Chepren; and their son, Devon, who slept in their car the night before in their quest to become the first guest family; they received lifetime passes to Disney theme parks worldwide for their efforts.

Park officials also paid tribute to an honorary first family—rhino crusader Michael Werikhe and his then-young daughters, Acacia and Kora—who were given a giant Key of Life (in the shape of the Tree of Life) at a ceremony inside the park, during which Roy E. Disney said:

> Michael Werikhe is one of the great eco-heroes of our time, thanks to his tireless efforts to walk the globe on behalf of the black rhino. With our honorary first family on hand, we invite all who cherish the striking beauty of animals and nature to venture out and witness the wonders that are here.

Rick Barongi added:

> They brought in the Rhino Man (Werikhe) when they opened the park and he touched everyone's heart. He was brought in by Roy Disney and I'll never forget it. The only name everybody knew at the time was Jane Goodall, but Disney (made animal conservationists) almost like rock stars.

In the weeks leading up to opening day, rumors were circulating that PETA, the animal rights organization, was planning to stage a protest at Animal Kingdom. A TV camera crew was stationed at the entrance to the park on the morning of opening day. The intent was to give PETA the chance to voice its opposition to the park under the guise of being interviewed by a real news reporter. After waiting in the parking lot for four hours, the faux TV crew packed up its gear and left, because PETA never showed.

What opening day guests witnessed was truly a remarkable transformation; a place that had gone from nondescript flatlands to a 500-acre "real-life Garden of Eden," as one first-time visitor called it. Disney's horticultural team, which included Bill Evans and his protégé, Paul Comstock, oversaw the planting of millions of trees and plants, which in turn became a lush jungle, flourishing forest, and vast savannah. Rivers, waterfalls and rock formations added to the sense the park had existed for decades.

Getting a place that's brand new to look as if it's aged and weather-beaten isn't easy, but it's a skill Disney's Imagineers have perfected.

The Harambe marketplace, for instance, offered opening day guests a "theater in which we invite our guests to experience Africa in a playful way," said Imagineer John Hench. Guests were "surrounded by wonderfully crafted artifacts and architecture in rich earth colors that complement the wildlife and the landscape." He explained that Disney artists had to be taught how to create the "aging process." According to Hench, some of the "best faux aging finishes" Disney has ever created can be seen at Animal Kingdom.

Marty Sklar said:

> One of my favorite aspects of the park is the paving. Wonderful things like animal tracks, leaves, tree roots. It adds to the feeling that you're in a different place.

"It's an art form," Walt Disney Imagineering's Diego Parras says proudly of the ability to make new things look old and distressed. It's also called attention to detail, a trait that Parras and his fellow Imagineers are downright fanatical about:

> On opening day, the walkways in Animal Kingdom looked like they had been there 30 or 40 years. We went

so far as to make leaf impressions in the cement along the walkways [as well as animal paw and hoof prints, tire tracks, cracks...even fake tree roots] and we made sure those impressions were from leaves from the trees growing in the immediate area.

Do Parras and his fellow Imagineers ever get frustrated knowing that many guests aren't taking in all the rich details they've worked so tirelessly to incorporate into every nook and cranny of the park?

Let's put it this way. They'd really miss all those details if we took them out.

Joe Rohde said:

We created this motif of age, of erosion. It reminds us that no matter how great our efforts, nature is the most powerful force around us, and we should respect it.

Attention to detail dates back to Disney's early animated works. Walt himself insisted that his artists learn everything they could about the real animals they were animating—how they walked, how they ran, how they ate, how they slept. On many occasions, live animals would be brought to the Disney studio in California where artists could study their movements from just a few feet away. Or the artists would visit zoos, sketch pads in hand.

Parras said:

The thing that sets Animal Kingdom apart from the other parks is this. Here, we're not trying to retell a classic story. This park is based on nature and all of its unpredictability. Here, you're in the moment, not making believe you're in a different time.

Rohde added:

Disney is all about storytelling. Only now, for the first time, real live animals are the storytellers—not as trained performers, but as fascinating families playing out real-life experiences on nature's landscape "stage."

According to Dr. Beth Stevens, who served as vice president of the park in its early days:

Kilimanjaro Safaris is easily Animal Kingdom's most expansive stage. Kilimanjaro Safaris demonstrates, absolutely, Disney's commitment to detail because it is so authentic. If you were to take pictures on the plains in Kenya and compare them to here, you wouldn't be able to tell the difference. It looks like Africa.

To many first-time Animal Kingdom visitors, getting up close and personal with a wide assortment of "wild animal storytellers" was the most enticing aspect of the park.

Guests arriving early on April 22 walked from either the parking lot tram drop-off point or the bus depot. To their left as they approached the main gate was a Disney parks first: a restaurant, Rainforest Café, fittingly known as a "wild place to shop and eat," was accessible from both outside and inside the park. The main gate featured an African-themed covering with the words "Disney's Animal Kingdom" centered above. The word "Disney's" was propped above an elephant's head, with its trunk coming between "Animal" and "Kingdom." Behind the name was a collage of marching animals.

A replica of Noah's Ark was among the initial proposals as a main gate concept, but quickly scrapped, in part because there were no mythical creatures on board the biblical wooden ship. Disney's designers went through several different concepts for the "opening scene" before settling on the Oasis, the only section of the park that has remained relatively unchanged over the past two decades. After the ark concept was scrapped, there was an idea to design a garden where animal statues would be placed to appear as if they, too, were walking into the park. "But we realized that all you'd see as you walked in were hundreds of animals' butts," Rohde said. A "Woodstocky"-type village with cottages and macramé and stained glass was considered, as was a cavernous grotto with ferns, but according to Rohde:

> The problem was, the grotto would have required 400,000 square feet of concrete to build the rockwork... probably all the cement you could find in Florida.

Finally, the idea for the Oasis took shape. It would capture the spirit of Animal Kingdom while "instantly establishing that this was a different place."

On that warm and sunny opening day, guests walked through the turnstiles and entered the Oasis, which served as a portal through which they'd passed to reach the exciting, one-of-a-kind adventures that lie ahead.

Rohde said:

> Nothing like Animal Kingdom exists anywhere in the world. Our guests journey into the last wild sanctuaries of the planet—vast forests and grasslands where the great herds of Africa will surround them. They meet nose to snout with fascinating creatures of all shapes and sizes. And they will race against time into the darkness of a prehistoric world where gigantic dinosaurs literally shake the earth around them.

Two decades later, the Oasis remains a tropical, shaded garden with two pathways leading into the park proper. The areas around the paths are populated with colorful birds and many different species of small mammals and reptiles. It starts just a few feet from the main gate, where pink flamingos stick their long legs into small ponds, all under the cover of shade trees. As guests walk along either of the winding paths, accentuated by the calming sounds of streams and waterfalls, they are greeted by a stunning collection of rare animals, most just a few feet away behind unobtrusive fences. Miniature deer, anteaters, sloths, tree kangaroos, blue and gold macaws, and iguanas were on hand for opening day, to be joined over the first few weeks by opportunistic ducks from the area who just couldn't pass up a free meal.

It's not unusual for guests to stop by and watch as keepers feed and tend to the birds and animals under their care. And it's also not unusual for guests to ask the keepers questions about the animals they're tending to. The Oasis is a table-setter, in that once inside the park, an even greater assortment of unique animal experiences awaits. Up ahead, there are two exploration trails, where gorillas and tigers can be viewed in a natural habitat; a bird and reptile sanctuary; a safari through a stunning savannah that's awash with a wide variety of species, many of whom walk without fear within a few feet of the safari vehicle; and a train ride to a conservation area where guests watch animals being cared for by skilled veterinarians.

Disney executive Michael Colglazier, who for a time was vice president of the park, said:

> Animal Kingdom is a different park. It is firmly grounded
> in connecting people with animals. And it's the kind of
> place where you should definitely take your time to enjoy
> its full impact.

Rohde added:

> As much as Animal Kingdom is a place, it is conceptual-
> ized as a story, with physical objects and people wrapped
> up inside the story. The best way to get value from
> Animal Kingdom is to slow down and read the story.

While opening-day guests were wildly appreciative of the
new park and receptive to just about every design element,
there was one flaw that had to be tweaked during the first few
weeks of operation. According to Marty Sklar, when Animal
Kingdom opened "we realized we had made a basic mistake
and the result was confusion for our early guests to the park."

"We wanted the park to feel adventurous," Rohde said. One
of the techniques the Imagineers employed in hopes of achieving that spirit of adventure was to block the view of what was
ahead, mostly by curving the narrow pathways which, in turn,
obscured the destination. Instead of a feeling of adventure,
there was just a sense of being lost.

Sklar said:

> I've often talked about the mistakes we made [at Animal
> Kingdom], including trying to keep everything like it was
> a mystery, so the walkways were narrow and winding
> and everything was hidden [when the park opened].
> People got confused, so we had to open things up. They
> needed a target, or a wienie, to set their sights on.

CHAPTER FIVE

Safari Village / Discovery Island

From the Oasis, opening-day guests walked up an incline, under stone archways, and over the first of five bridges that spanned Discovery River and linked Safari Village to the rest Animal Kingdom (a sixth bridge now connects Asia to the area which is home to the Theater in the Wild). As guests entered Safari Village—which served the dual purpose of being the park's hub and its own unique version of Main Street, U.S.A.—the stunning Tree of Life loomed large and majestically up ahead. It was—and still is—a great photo opportunity. In true Disney hub-and-spoke fashion, Safari Village gave guests a departure point where they could head off to other park adventures in themed lands—Camp Minnie-Mickey, Africa, Conservation Station, a still-under-construction Asia, and DinoLand U.S.A.

Upon entering Safari Village, guests were greeted by wide walkways and animal-inspired artwork, with bright, vivid colors and festive architecture setting the mood. Disney's creative staff was aiming for a tropical artists' colony...and they succeeded. It was truly a collaborative effort: Dave Minichiello did concept renderings to establish the look; architect Gerry Dunn designed most of Safari Village's buildings; Ahmad Jafari was responsible for reducing the buildings' scale; Joe Rohde designed most of the 1,500 wooden animal carvings; and Jenna Frere (now Goodman) did the color on all the animal motifs. The animal carvings were the handiwork of dozens of skilled craftsmen from Bali.

Safari Village shops, with names such as Beastly Bazaar, Creature Comforts, Disney Outfitters, and Island Mercantile, added to the buoyant atmosphere, as did several cleverly named and heavily themed restaurants, including Flame Tree Barbecue and Pizzafari.

The decor inside Pizzafari is a show unto itself, with animal murals covering the walls and colorful animal figurines adorning the ceilings. The murals were designed by Frank Armitage, an Australian-born artist and active member of Doctors Without Borders, who first began working for the Walt Disney Company in 1952. His film portfolio is extensive and impressive, with artistic contributions to *Lady and the Tramp*, *Peter Pan*, *Sleeping Beauty*, *Mary Poppins*, and *The Jungle Book*. He transferred to Walt Disney Imagineering in 1977 and worked on several theme park projects, including the Wonders of Life pavilion at Epcot and the Pizzafari murals, which designer Zofia Kostyrko calls "some of the most clever and beautiful animal picture stories and stylized original animal designs in the park." Armitage's wife Karen and daughter Nicole also were Imagineers. Nicole, in fact, painted her father's murals in Pizzafari.

Unlike a typical Disney Main Street, however, all the buildings in Safari Village are one story and low to the ground, giving guests a relatively unobstructed view of the surrounding thickly treed areas. The use of "forced perspective," so prevalent in many Disney architectural park designs, wouldn't come into play in Animal Kingdom until Expedition Everest debuted in 2006.

Joe Rohde said:

> Safari Village is like no place on Earth, it's a place where the love of animals bursts out across walls and rooftops, as folk-art carvings and colorful paintings. Balinese wood carvers spent two years producing hundreds of artistic pieces that adorn our village.

More than 50 artisans from Bali crafted the carvings, which were placed on Safari Village's buildings to give a whimsical flair—as well as stunning bursts of color—to the area. It's a fusion of world folk art, gaining inspiration from pre-Colombian, Peruvian, African, and Polynesian styles. Unlike the replicated villages in the Africa and Asia sections of the park, which were modeled after existing towns, Safari Village doesn't exist in the real world and so has its own unique qualities.

Zofia Kostyrko, who was a member of the park's original design and concept team, made contributions to Safari Village, designing some of the architectural and animals motifs. She began her Disney career in 1987, although she admits she was reluctant to do so:

> Actually, me joining Imagineering was a complete fluke. I was a fine artist and a costume designer and I went to the Art Center College of Design in Pasadena to become an illustrator and a fine artist. Then I was doing film production design. I was working on *Pee Wee's Playhouse*. A friend of mine told me about an opening at this place called Imagineering. She said, "You should interview for it. You'd be perfect for it." And I said, "I'm not interested. I'm doing *Pee Wee's Playhouse* and I'm doing film production and that's what I want to do." But she convinced me to check it out.

Ms. Kostyrko went for an interview and met several people, including Peggy Van Pelt, who was in charge of nurturing and building the talent pool at Imagineering:

> Basically, I was planning to be there a year only, because I thought it would be fun to do for just a little bit. It turned out to be 13 years. I was immediately pulled into the Rick Rothschild design group, handling all the entertainment centers. My first project was Pleasure Island [in Downtown Disney]. I worked on Mannequins and the Adventurers Club with Joe Rohde. That was quite amazing.

Her work on the Adventurers Club was somewhat prescient. The theme of the club? A tongue-in-cheek outpost for weary wildlife explorers who had returned from safari. She also helped design Body Wars and Frontiers of Medicine for the Wonders of Life pavilion at Epcot. "There were very few women working doing concepts at the time, but I always had a great time working with the guys."

Then fate, in the form of a communique from Imagineering leader Marty Sklar, intervened:

> Basically, Marty put out a call to the whole company, asking for folks in concept and show design to come up

with ideas for Animal Kingdom. I came up with 15 ideas
and Joe Rohde picked me as the first designer on the team.
There were five or six of us [on the team] at the start.

If you are familiar with Joe's work, he has his own way
on how to develop a concept and I'm the same way. Build
a very strong conceptual core, and as you know, the
concept of Animal Kingdom is love of animals. You have
the child's love, which are the stories and fairy tales, the
teenage love, which is the thrill of adventures, and you
have the mature love, which is the knowledge. It took
a long time to distill it.

The Tree of Life is, of course, the main attention-grabber
in Safari Village, both as the park's icon and as a featured
show: under the Tree of Life's massive "root" system is an
Imagineering tour-de-force, a show called It's Tough to Be a Bug.

From a distance, the Tree of Life stands out, but still
blends seamlessly with the other trees that surround it. Upon
closer inspection, though, the tree "comes to life"—its bark
and root system is enhanced by 325 carved animals of all
shapes, sizes, and species. Included in the artistic menagerie
at the tree's base are an alligator, an armadillo, an elephant,
a camel, a baboon, and a silverback gorilla. It took 20 artists
and hundreds of assistants, all led by chief sculptor and senior
production manager Zsolt Hormay, 18 months of painstaking effort to create this stunning work of art. Skip Lange
was the show producer; the sculptors included Vinnie Byrne,
Fabrice Kennel, Eric Kovach, Steve Humke, Joe Welborn, Gary
Bondurant, Jacob Eaddy, Roger White, Patrick Boyiddle, Craig
Goseyun, and Arthur Rowlodge.

Hormay said:

> The most difficult part of sculpting was to create animal
> figures that appear to be formed of bark and wood.
> Finding the balance between animal forms and wood
> textures was a great challenge.

The sculpting was handled by some of the best artisans in
the world, from Ireland, France, California, and Florida. Some
of them were Native Americans who carved animals that were
part of their tribal identity.

Zofia Kostryko said:

> That universal, almost spiritual connection we all had to the subject matter makes the Tree of Life even more of a genuine and immense piece of fine art than it already is...and that is what makes it truly unique.

Added Hormay:

> We want visitors to recognize animals and seek out others. [Viewing the Tree of Life is] a constant discovery and rediscovery.

The Tree of Life wasn't the first man-made tree in a Disney park. The Swiss Family Treehouse in the Magic Kingdom at Walt Disney World and Tarzan's Treehouse in Disneyland have been entertaining guests for decades. What's the difference between the Swiss Family/Tarzan treehouses—known unofficially as *Disneyodendron eximus*, or "out of the ordinary Disney tree"—and the Tree of Life? The Swiss Family/Tarzan creations are walkthroughs (or more accurately, a walk-*up*; it takes 116 steps to climb to the top). Along the way, guests see how the Robinsons and Tarzan from the classic books and Disney films lived. The Swiss Family/Tarzan treehouses are made of steel, concrete, and stucco, and weigh 200 tons. They are covered with 300,000 polyethylene leaves and have 1,400 branches. The Tree of Life has 103,000 leaves—all attached by hand—and more than 8,000 branches. It's 160 feet wide and 145 feet tall.

Like any form of plant life on Earth, "bugs" have managed to worm their way under the Tree of Life. According to Joe Rohde, the It's Tough to be a Bug show was another daunting assignment for Disney's creative staff:

> The challenge for us was to come up with a show on the inside of the Tree of Life that would capture the spirit and magnificence of the outside.

To that end, Disney's Imagineers turned to the world of insects for inspiration...and to an Imagineer who didn't much care for bugs in the first place.

Show producer Kevin Rafferty explained:

> I've been totally fearful of insects my entire life. It's kind of weird, the things I've worked on, like Tower of Terror, the original one...I have a fear of falling; Rock N Roller

Coaster...I don't like to go upside down; It's Tough to Be
a Bug...I have this phobia of bugs! I guess I'm the right
person to be doing all this stuff.

Like most Disney attractions, It's Tough to be a Bug took
a circuitous route from early concepts to finished attraction.

Rafferty said:

When Animal Kingdom was being developed, the outside
structure of the Tree of Life was going to be like the
castle and the base of the tree was going to be a walkthrough, like the castles are. I was at a meeting one day
and [then-Disney chairman and CEO] Michael Eisner
asked, "Is the base of the tree big enough to put a show
in?" And we said, "Yeah, we could probably put a couple
hundred seats in that thing," and it changed the whole
design of that. He tasked me to come up with a show to
put inside that. At that time, *The Lion King* was big and
Rafiki was the wise old sage and all that, so I came up
with a show that had Rafiki as an Audio-Animatronics
character, talking about the animal kingdom.

I pitched the idea to Michael and he said, "You know,
that's really a good show. If it were at any other place than
Animal Kingdom, it would be a 10, but it's really only an
8 on a scale of 1 to 10 and it's really got to be spectacular.

Coincidentally, Pixar Animation Studios was working on
a movie about bugs (*A Bug's Life*) at the time. Eisner suggested
that Rafferty get in touch with the folks at Pixar:

I thought, 'My gosh, where did that come from?'
I thought he was crazy! Why would Michael suggest a
show about bugs when this is a park about animals? So
I started to do research and the first book I found said
on the first page, "The 10 quintillion insects of the world
comprise 80 percent of the animal kingdom." I thought,
'Man that is fantastic!' I had to put my fear of bugs aside,
because without them, we'd be in a world of hurt.

In further researching the project, Rafferty came upon
a live-action/cartoon featurette in the Disney vaults called *It's
Tough to Be a Bird*, released in 1969 and was directed by anima-
tor Ward Kimball, who was noted as a bit of a lovable oddball.

The main storyline showed the bird's contribution to mankind and its constant struggle for survival. *It's Tough to Be a Bird* "was kind of the inspiration of the whole thing," Rafferty said of It's Tough to be a Bug, adding:

> We try to do "edu-tainment." We try to put a little education into our shows. The bug show was kind of a takeoff on *It's Tough to Be a Bird*. As far as the research went, I started to meet with some entomologists, even some entomologists from the Smithsonian Institution. Of course, we wanted to make it as entertaining a 3D show as possible. I was asking them about what kind of interesting things that real bugs do in nature that we could put in the show to support the theme that it really is tough to be a bug. What do those guys need to do to survive? There was a session with some entomologists and they said, "You know, there are soldier termites that spray acid on their prey," and I thought, 'Man, there's a 3D act!' "And there's Chilean tarantulas that throw poison quills at their prey," and I was like, 'Wow! This thing is writing itself!'

Rafferty said that although Pixar and its creative leader, John Lasseter, were working on *A Bug's Life*, they were still years away from releasing it in theaters:

> They didn't really have a whole lot of time to work on our show with us, so essentially, I was given permission to make up my own characters, the rule being that they had to be believable, that if they were in the movie, they'd look the same. All Pixar had at the time were Flik the ant and Hopper the grasshopper. Those were the first characters they had developed; the other ones were still evolving, so we got to use Flik and Hopper, which was fantastic, and all the other bug characters we got to make up, all exclusive to It's Tough to Be a Bug. This is one of the few attractions, I think, that Imagineering's ever done where the characters in an attraction predated the release of the movie. I think the show opened six weeks before the premiere of *A Bug's Life*, so we got to introduce [Flik and Hopper] before the movie came out. That doesn't happen frequently because it takes so much time to develop an attraction.

Since opening day, It's Tough to Be a Bug has been shown continuously throughout the day in a theater that seats 430 guests wearing "bug-eye" 3D glasses. Guests enter the underground queue area and are greeted by rather humorous Broadway-style posters.

Rafferty explained:

> The posters were just a fun opportunity to communicate that this was a Bugway production, like Broadway. So, to set that story up, we thought it would be great to put these parodies of Broadway posters, like "A Cockroach Line," "My Fair Lady Bug," "Barefoot in the Bark," and "Beauty and the Bees," that kind of stuff. Essentially, that's what that was for, to show that this was a Bugway show and these were the other productions that happened to play in this theater over the years.

In addition to Flik and Hopper and the other characters created specifically for the show, there's a montage of 1950s-era film clips showing how bugs have been mistreated and misunderstood over the years. Among the highlights of the show that had guests buzzing were the appearance of Hopper, the chief protagonist of the movie and an Audio-Animatronics marvel; a stink bug's untimely release of a rather offensive odor; and another bug squirting a presumed "poisonous acid" into the audience. It's all topped off when a crawly creature appears to have taken up residence...on your seat!

According to Rafferty, Hopper was among the most complex Audio-Animatonics figures ever developed by Imagineering:

> With all the little spindly grasshopper tentacles, it was hard to do. We, as an audience, shrink down to the size of a bug, so Hopper had to be relatively the same scale as he was in the film. Plus, he was designed to come up on a lift that brings him up to the show, in a couple of seconds. All of that carriage and all that complexity of the entire figure as it came up on the lift was a real challenge. What's really great about the team here is they really rise to the occasion. All the complexities of that Hopper figure... there was a lot of head-scratching going on, but somehow, they figured out how it all came together...going up and down as it does during the show cycles.

And then there was the stink bug effect:

> The special-effects guys actually put a stink bug in a sandwich bag and wanted to know if we wanted it to be that smell, and we said, "No, no. We want it to be something a little less pungent." Tom Fitzgerald was one of the creative leads at the time and his guys would come in and let us smell some of the stink bug effects they came up with. After a while, it was like, "Oh, no. Here they come again!" Finally, we landed on the top three smells and we left it to [Animal Kingdom creative leader] Joe Rohde to decide. The one that's in the theater now is the one he picked. He said, "This is great. This is *earthy!*"

Rafferty claims that the "butt-bug" effect was his idea:

> It's always fun to leave our guests happy and laughing and getting a surprise that they totally didn't expect. Just to bring it all home with a smile. When I open an attraction, I like to sit or ride through with guests right after it opens to just kind of hear what they say and how they react to it and stuff. I remember when the park opened, I sat down at one of the first shows. There was this elderly couple sitting right in front of me halfway back in the audience. They had to be in their late 80s and they screamed and yelled and had a great time when that little butt bug went by. When everyone stood up to leave the theater, the husband turned to the wife and said, "I don't know what that was, but I want to do that again!"

As guests are exiting the theater, the song "We're Pollinators" comes over the speakers:

> We knew we wanted to do kind of a finale song because it was kind of a Broadway-esque type show, so at one of my meetings with the entomologists, I made sure to ask them, "If you were to tell our guests important things about the importance of bugs, what would it be?" One of them said, "If it wasn't for the fact that they pollinate, human beings wouldn't be around on this planet very long." And another one said, "Yeah, and if bugs didn't eliminate waste, the same thing would happen." So

basically, the two most important things from the ento-
mologists' point of view was to communicate to guests
that unless bugs pollinate and unless bugs eliminated
waste, we wouldn't be around too long, and that's how
the finale song came to be. I wrote the finale and that's
where the pollinators' song came about and that was
kind of fun. A real message to get across. I wrote the
lyrics and George Wilkins wrote the music.

We're pollinators!
We're pollinators!
If you like vegetables, fresh fruits, and flowers,
Give thanks to us bugs for our marvelous powers!
If it weren't for the fact that we like the taste,
You'd be out there wallowing in shoulder-high waste!
Shoulder-high waste!
And if all bugs were wiped off the face of the planet,
There'd soon be no humans around here to man it.
The best thing about us: you can't live without us!
Still, it's tough to be a bug!

It was the kind of rousing song-and-dance finale that
would have made legendary Broadway show producer Busby
Berkeley proud.

The area around the Tree of Life's massive structure—
known since opening day as the Tree of Life Garden—serves
as a mini-wildlife reserve. Woven into the landscape are
pools, meadows, a waterfall, and lush greenery. Built into
this pristine area is a natural habitat for small, often colorful animals—flamingos, blue-and-yellow macaws, Galapagos
tortoises, and Red kangaroos. Playful otters can be seen above
ground and in an underground viewing area.

Also in Safari Village on opening day were the Discovery
River Boats, whose intent was to offer guests a "grand-cir-
cle tour" of the park's many different lands, much like the
Disneyland or Walt Disney World railroads. Prior to the park's
opening, the attraction consisted of just a boat ride through
a lush landscape. Michael Eisner took a ride on the boat
pre-opening and asked for changes. "It's a pretty sight," he said
after getting off the boat, "but what is the intellectual content?

What could we do to make it exciting?" What was done was to create a Jungle Cruise-type boat ride that featured humorous anecdotes about life on the river as told by explorer/guides.

Guests boarded the canopied launches from Safari Village or from the Upcountry Landing at Harambe off the shores of the Africa section of the park. The boats sailed around Discovery River and under stone bridges linking Safari Village to the rest of the park. Among the highlights of the scenic excursion (in addition to the Jungle Cruise-type spiel given by the boats' skippers) was coming across a 30-foot-tall Audio-Animatronics iguanodon, which paused from grazing on reeds at the river's edge to rear up on its hind legs to greet the boats. There also was an encounter with Dragon Rocks, where a fire-breathing dragon was said to be waiting. Indeed, singed knights' armor littered the area, and menacing sounds and bursts of fire came from the rocks, heightening the experience.

On the wider section of Discovery River, between Asia and DinoLand U.S.A., was a display of floating animal fountains called Aquanimals.

According to Zofia Kostyrko:

> They were kinetic steel sculptures, beautifully painted, their moving parts propelled and partially shaped by water jets and streams animating the figures. Water was also creating insect wings, fish fins and fish tails, and the expanding frill and scrambling toes of a lizard. There were goldfish, a dragonfly and butterfly with lily pad floating tanks perched on a reed.

There also was a basilisk lizard, the so-called Jesus Christ lizard...because he can walk on water.

During the boat ride, skippers showed guests a variety of menacing-looking bugs (leaches and tarantulas) to help broaden their knowledge.

Eisner said of the modest upgrades:

> It's expensive. You're adding an extra person on the boat, and there are a lot of boats. But it's worth it.

Despite those last-minute changes, however, the Discovery River Boats were a short-lived attraction; they closed about a year after the park opened.

Marty Sklar explained:

> We had the same thing in the Magic Kingdom, with the Swan Boats. They didn't really get a big play because people didn't want to sit on a long boat ride with not a lot to see, except for vegetation. And it wasn't appropriate to do the same kind of spiel you have on the Jungle Cruise because this park is filled with serious stuff. We wanted it to be fun, but we also had to be serious, as we should be with real animals.

The river boats' colorful—and covered—boat docks have been used as character photo spots since the boats were grounded. And, like the river boats, the name Safari Village became extinct at the end of the year 2000 in favor of Discovery Island. The original Discovery Island—the one located in Bay Lake across from the Contemporary Resort—had shut down by that time, freeing up the name to be used at Animal Kingdom.

Afternoon parades have been a regular feature at Disney theme parks since Disneyland opened in the mid-1950s. Animal Kingdom had a parade of its own on opening day, the March of the Animals, which was held on the pathways around Safari Village. The parade celebrated animals with a procession that combined humor, music, and modern art—which was apropos, considering that Safari Village was themed to be an artists' colony. The parade, in fact, showcased the talents of Safari Village's painters, sculptors, basket-makers, weavers, papier-mache makers, and costume designers.

A total of 55 performers took part in the March of the Animals, most dressed in costumes designed in the shapes of animals, including frogs, storks, alligators, and elephants. The procession featured musicians, acrobats, dancers, and stilt-walkers. Over the years, the afternoon parade has been updated, most notably, the Jammin' Jungle Parade. There even was a parade shown in the weeks prior to Christmas that was themed to the holidays, called the Jingle Jungle Parade.

On the outskirts of Discovery Island, visible to guests as they walk toward Pandora: The World of Avatar, is a new signature restaurant that has drawn rave reviews since opening in 2016. Tiffins (and the accompanying Nomad Lounge, which overlooks Discovery River) is an Imagineering tour-de-force, simply because it serves as an homage to the original design team and their research travels. Just inside the restaurant's main door is a plaque that sums up Tiffins' mission:

> Tiffins is a gallery of art based on the travels and adventures that inspired the creation of Disney's Animal Kingdom.

Joe Rohde said:

> Tiffins was inspired by the Imagineers' travels. It is both a restaurant and an art gallery. Each piece of art in Tiffins talks about travel, adventure, and collaboration.

To take it a step further, in addition to the stunning artwork on display, affixed to the walls are actual drawings, photos, and notes from members of the design team made during their travels to Africa, Asia, and South America in the years leading up to Animal Kingdom's debut. As you might expect, Tiffins' lunch and dinner offerings are eclectic and exotic.

Opening Day Attractions in Safari Village

Highlights: Tree of Life, Tree of Life Garden, It's Tough to Be a Bug, Discovery River Boats at Safari Village

Dining: Flame Tree Barbecue, Pizzafari

Shopping: Beastly Bazaar, Creature Comforts, Disney Outfitters, Island Mercantile

Current Attractions on Discovery Island

Highlights: Tree of Life, Tree of Life Garden, Adventurers Outpost, It's Tough to Be a Bug, Wilderness Explorers

Dining: Flame Tree Barbecue, Pizzafari, Eight Spoon Café, Smiling Crocodile, Isle of Java, Tiffins, Nomad Lounge, Terra Treats

Shopping: Island Mercantile, Riverside Depot, Discovery Trading Company

CHAPTER SIX

Africa

Most Disney parks guests tend to be in a big hurry. They're either power-walking their way to a popular attraction or show or they're trying to arrive at a restaurant as the clock ticks down on their reservation time. It's a sad fact that many of those heads-down, legs-furiously-pumping guests don't stop to smell the roses...or take in the incredible details Disney's Imagineers have worked tirelessly to embed in everything they do.

Case in point: the village of Harambe, which serves as the entry portal to the Africa section of Animal Kingdom.

Harambe, which means "coming together," is modeled after the type of port village you'd see in East Africa. The level of detail is astonishing. What was new on opening day appeared to be decidedly old and weather-beaten—tattered-looking stucco and exposed brickwork; slouching telephone poles with low-slung wires stretching across the main courtyard; fading (and often humorous) signs and posters; parked bicycles, rusted and worn down; and an aging baobab tree at the outskirts of the town. Making buildings look decades old is one thing; making them look old while adhering to Florida's strict building codes is quite another. Disney's artisans did a masterful job of combining the old look with new construction methods. Harambe's buildings were designed by architects Eli Erlandson, Tom Sze, and Ahmad Jafari. Character plasterers, under the direction of John Olson, were responsible for the unique textures on each of the structures.

In the heart of Harambe, as it has been since opening day, is Tusker House, one of the park's signature restaurants and the venue for one of Walt Disney World's more popular character breakfasts. The interior of the restaurant is designed in hub-and-spoke fashion: the many African-inspired buffet food selections are located in a circular center court, with dining rooms fanning out from there. Also in Harambe on opening day was the Tamu Tamu Refreshment Stand and a few souvenir shops, all themed perfectly to blend in with the East African coastal setting. Indeed, near the river banks to either side of the bridge leading to Harambe are signs of everyday village life—small wooden boats docked on the water's edge, fishing gear, and cargo boxes.

Among the authentic architectural elements featured in Harambe are hand-made thatched roofs which, Disney discovered during the design phase of the park, are difficult to replicate. Finding the proper materials also proved problematic. In its constant quest for authenticity, Disney took the unprecedented step of going right to the source—Africa, where they obtained 15 trailer loads of thatch, which consist of hand-harvested Berg, as well as battens. Berg thatching grass is known to resist insects and decay while providing insulation; the battens, used to secure the thatch to the hardwood rafters, are made from eucalyptus wood.

Disney also enlisted 13 Zulu craftsmen from the Kwazulu/Natal area in South Africa. They worked barefoot during the thatching process, as they were used to doing (the craftsmen had to obtain a waiver from the U.S. Occupational Safety and Health Administration to work barefoot). The group made three separate trips to central Florida to work on the roofs, and what they created on the buildings' rooftops was not only authentic, but extremely durable, with a life expectancy in Florida's blazing sun and often torrential rain of about 60 years.

On any given day since the park opened, live entertainment has been a key component of Harambe's appeal. Dancers and musicians, always dressed in colorful African garb, perform on a regular basis. You're just as likely to hear a traditional African song as you are to hear "He Lives in You" from *The Lion King*. Most guests will stop, watch, and listen for a few minutes, then move on, but it's always time well spent.

There were a variety of hidden gems in Harambe that contributed to its sense of being a realistic experience. During the park's early years, master carver David Masuko, a native of

Kenya, crafted hand-carved treasures in full view of the park's guests at a kiosk outside of the Mombasa Marketplace merchandise store. As they watched in awe, Masuko carved wood figurines and masks out of cedar, ebony teak, and mahogany, a process that carried on a proud family tradition.

On opening day, Africa's main attraction—and, indeed, the heart of Animal Kingdom's mission of teaching conservation while celebrating animals—was Kilimanjaro Safaris, where 32-passenger, open-air safari trucks traversed a rugged, two-mile long roadway into a lush green forest, then across rivers and waterfalls to the magnificent Serengeti grasslands. In all, there are 44 safari vehicles at the ready at Animal Kingdom, each costing $250,000. The vehicles are covered, but open-sided, allowing guests a virtually unobstructed view of the lush landscape...and the wide assortment of animals who roam freely there. Unlike the Audio-Animatronics figures that permeate Disney parks, the stars of the savannah aren't controlled by state-of-the-art wizardry; they're real and they're in abundance.

Joe Rohde said:

> We're not talking about a couple of hippos here and there. There are large pods of hippos, herds of zebra, a pride of lions. And you are right there among them.

The roadways along Kilimanjaro Safaris were both a challenge and a triumph for Disney's creative team. Knowing full-well what a constant parade of heavy safari vehicles would do to a typical dirt road exposed to blazing sun or torrential rainfall, they came up with a strategy to create a realistic-looking "dirt" road made from concrete. First, they dyed the concrete to match the color of the dirt alongside the roads. Then, after pouring the concrete, they "weathered" the roadways by rolling tires over them before adding dirt, stones, and twigs. In addition, "pucks" were placed under the roadway to allow cast members in a central control room to monitor each vehicle along the route, ensuring that there wouldn't be a backup of vehicles at any point. The pucks "read" each truck as they pass over them, much like a barcode scanner at a supermarket, sending a signal back to the control room.

One of the most intriguing aspects of the Kilimanjaro Safaris is the fact that, although there might be as many as 30 trucks on safari at one time, only three or four are visible to guests. That's because the safari route was designed with elevation in land, stands of trees, or rockwork placed in such a way as to hide the other vehicles in view. In a real sense, Rohde explains, these obstructions act as walls between scenes:

> We give guests the illusion of a natural environment, but Kilimanjaro Safaris was designed just like Pirates of the Caribbean.

As with anything Disney does, Kilimanjaro Safaris is all about "the story"...in this case, it's the story of wild animals living in as natural a man-made habitat that's ever been created, all while guarding themselves against predators, both natural and human. And poachers. The experience began along the long queue area, where TV screens told the story of the savannah and the Harambe Wildlife Preserve where the animals lived. Then you climbed aboard the large safari vehicle, parked near a ranger station. Like just about everything else in Animal Kingdom, the safari vehicles appeared to have been in service for years. They carried weathered suitcases and water coolers and the sides of the vehicle were dented, rusted, and spattered with faux mud and animal droppings...just the way they'd look if you were going on an actual safari in Africa.

Your driver, who doubled as your guide, was in constant contact with a bush pilot named Wilson, who flew ahead to seek out animals of interest, all the while keeping a watchful eye out for poachers. Conversations between the driver and Wilson could be heard over the loudspeaker. During those conversations, Wilson referred to the vehicle as "Simba One." At times, music themed to Africa was piped in over the speakers. The vehicle rumbled out of the loading area and headed out into a thick, green forest, populated by antelope and okapi. Farther along, hippos lounged in large pools of water and a colony of colobus monkeys frolicked nearby. As the truck made its way over a rickety bridge, guests were taken aback by the dozens of Nile crocodiles sunning themselves in the water *just a few feet below.*

Safe for now, the truck rolled out into the vast savannah, where an entire new collection of animals awaited. Giraffes and zebras stood out, but on closer inspection, you could spot wildebeests, warthogs, and Thomson's gazelles. ("No, no, no. They're called Tommies...Tommies"! Wilson admonished.) Up ahead were watering holes where birds of different feathers—East Africa crowned cranes, ostriches, hornbills, and Great Flamingos—flocked together. All the animals and birds roamed freely through the trees and grasslands, with no visible barriers or fences. They also were provided settings which encourage them to behave naturally, such as wallows for rolling and pools for swimming. Apart from the tall grasses, the landscape was punctuated by odd-looking trees, including acacia and sausage trees, where foot-long seed pods shaped like sausages dangled from the limbs. Termite mounds, some up to 20 feet high, also could be seen.

What couldn't be seen, hidden behind downed tree limbs and stumps, were containers filled with fresh water and food. As challenging as it was for Disney's design team to create buildings that looked aged and weathered, it was a monumental task for the animal staff to get the creatures to behave on cue while "performing" for the excited guests looking on. One of the more innovative ways to feed giraffes on the savannah while keeping them within camera range was to incorporate a lazy Susan-type device into an artificial baobab tree. A timer was affixed to the lazy Susan so that it rotated ever so slowly. Tasty (to giraffes, anyway) acacia leaves were placed there to entice them to spend a good part of their day near the trees.

Paul Comstock explained:

> That way, when people come by in the ride vehicles, there's Mr. and Mrs. Giraffe staring right in their faces, because the plants they like to eat—the candy, the Godiva chocolate of the plant world—are right there for the photo op. Bingo!

After exiting the savannah, the safari truck entered an area where elephants walked within massive rock formations. They walked about slowly, but confidently, having learned over time that natural and human predators are no longer a threat. The elephants are among Animal Kingdom's most voracious eaters, each consuming 125 pounds of food per day. Elephants are highly intelligent and communicate with one another. They can live up to 60 years and members of each herd are bonded, so much so that when a member of the herd dies, the remaining members will mourn its death.

Also seen in this section of the safari are magnificent black and white rhinos, who have been known to stride within a few feet of the truck—or stop altogether—making for some spectacular photo opportunities...as well as some anxious moments. In a real sense, however, it's good to see so many of the imposing creatures moving about: their species is critically endangered. At Animal Kingdom, safe from predators, hippos will consume 30–40 pounds of food a day, mostly hay and romaine lettuce.

Near the end of the motor tour, male and female lions could be spotted sitting majestically atop a hill, looking down on the kingdom they reign over, not too unlike the lions who frequent Pride Rock in *The Lion King*. They are the penultimate attraction of the safari.

During Kilimanjaro Safaris' first few years, the journey culminated with the rescue of several endangered elephants—Audio-Animatronics creatures named Big Red and Little Red—from poachers. Near the end of the safari, Wilson would inform the driver that there were poachers ahead who had wounded Big Red and apparently captured Little Red. Then Wilson asked if we'd help in rescuing the two endangered elephants. Of course, the answer was always yes and a hot pursuit of the poachers commenced. Our vehicle picked up speed as we headed to a gorge, the sounds of gunshots and bullets glancing off the side of the vehicle interspersed with the radio communique: "We're going after them!" Several harrowing minutes later, the vehicle would drive past a makeshift camp, where elephant tusks were scattered on the ground. Finally, the pilot radioed a welcome message: "We've landed. The rangers are here and the poachers are in custody!" And, most importantly, Little Red and his mother had been rescued.

Although that storyline has changed, the lengthy excursion through the magnificent savannah remains a must-see for park guests, one that was enhanced in 2015 with the introduction of a safari in the shadows of darkness.

At the end of a typical day at Kilimanjaro Safaris, after the last safari truck has rumbled back to the loading area and guests exit the park, Animal Kingdom's staff of more than 150 animal curators, managers and workers takes center stage. It's during this time that most of the animals are "called" back to shelters, in part for their own security, but also to receive individualized care and treatment, if needed. The animals are conditioned to respond to a sound devised just for them. For instance, when a cowbell is rung, zebras will dutifully make their way from the savannah to their shelters. Giraffes return upon hearing a coach's whistle, while a goose call gets the attention of Thompson's gazelles...make that Tommies!

The training process was painstaking and took months before the animal keepers began to see results. When the animals were brought to Animal Kingdom from accredited zoos around America about a year before the park opened, they were first introduced to their shelters. In time, they were allowed access to the areas just outside the shelters. Finally, using temporary fencing, they were encouraged to make their way out to the grasslands or forests. The animals learned to walk from the shelters "backstage" to the areas visible to guests "onstage." Only after they learned to return to the shelters upon hearing their specific call were the fences removed. As with any animal behavioral training techniques, the animals were rewarded as they progressed through the desired behaviors. Those rewards were as varied as the animal species themselves: rhinos prefer apples, hippos love carrots, and giraffes are fond of carrots and lettuce.

Rick Barongi, the park's director of Animal Project Development, said:

> Some of the animals came here with a routine like that already. Some animals came from smaller enclosures [and were easier to train]. Sometimes we got animals that were in big areas that didn't go in at night at all. Marty Sevenich [the park's curator of Behavioral Husbandry] was a key to that. She came from the Brookfield Zoo [near Chicago]. I found her. She was such a good keeper. Many of the keepers didn't know how to do that [enrichment conditioning]. After a while, at a certain time of day, the animals would know when to come in. When the clock changes, they'd get a little screwed up. We had

a team of people doing [the animal training]. We had to train the keepers before we could train the animals.

The other featured attraction in Africa, the Pangani Forest Exploration Trail, remains to this day a pleasant and educational respite (though with a different name: Gorilla Falls Exploration Trail). Guests who exited Kilimanjaro Safaris could extend their adventure by walking along the heavily treed, animal-rich trail. The highlight along the winding, shaded path was [and still is] undoubtedly the majestic silverback gorillas, seen in a natural, safe setting. The gorillas will often munch on tree branches while sitting in the shade, or they'll walk slowly around rocks and stumps, or they'll simply sit and stare back in curiosity at the delighted humans on the other side of a small chasm which serves as a natural barrier.

Along the trail, guests also viewed, up close, a stunning collection of birds, fish, amphibians, and insects. At each stop, trained keepers answered any questions guests might have had.

The first stop along the trail was a scientific research station, made from large wood beams. Inside, a glass wall revealed a series of tunnels dug by naked mole rats. After passing through a screen door, guests entered a giant, mesh-covered aviary, where many rare tropical birds flitted about. At ground level, large pools housed frogs, turtles, iguanas, and rare fish. After exiting the aviary, guests found themselves face to face with several hippos, seen either floating above or below the water line thanks to an inch-thick glass barrier. Up ahead after the hippo area was a circular savannah overlook, where a variety of animals could be seen grazing on tall grasses. In the hippo viewing area, the Imagineers put on display the original drawings made by children in Africa who were participating in the conservation and education program "Roots and Shoots," which was founded by Jane Goodall.

Zofia Kostyrko noted:

> The attention to detail and tangible connection with the real world—real places and real people, their stories and their work—always is present throughout Animal Kingdom, unlike any other Disney destination.

Finally, guests came upon the gorillas, which could be viewed from either a glass enclosure or in a natural setting, complete with a swaying suspension bridge which bisected a colony of bachelors and a family (two females, one silverback, and their offspring). It was usually at this spot where guests would stop, quietly observe, and snap dozens of photos of the majestic primates in their rolling, forest-like setting.

Africa has seen significant expansion over the past few years. The new Festival of the Lion King venue and a large restroom facility nearby were added to Harambe and blended seamlessly into the area's theming, as did the most recent addition to the area, Harambe Market. The market includes Kitamu Grill, featuring skewered chicken and a kebab flat-bread sandwich; Famous Sausages (corndogs made with South African boerewors sausage); Chef Mwanga's (featuring spice-rubbed Karubi Rib); and Wanjohi's Refreshments (offering an assortment of craft beers, wines, and other cool drinks, with or without alcohol). All four themed shops replicate the look and feel of a traditional African street market.

To achieve this authenticity, Disney's Imagineers—in keeping with Animal Kingdom's "boots on the ground" tradition—made research trips to Africa to learn the intricacies of local cuisine. They also worked closely with Disney's food and beverage team to develop foods comparable to what can be found in Africa.

Chef Lenny DeGeorge explained:

> These foods have been tailored for the locals. With the ribs, we have a ras el hanout spice blend, which has about 20 different spices mixed in. The berbere spice is on the chicken skewer and the kebab sandwich. We used madras curry powder in the corndog batter.

The Harambe Market is located near the entrance to Kilimanjaro Safaris and the Wildlife Express Train Station. In fact, the train is now visible from the market as it makes its regular runs to Rafiki's Plant Watch.

Walt Disney Imagineering art director Joan Hartwig said:

> For Harambe Market, we had the opportunity to travel in East Africa and bring back details that our guests will be able to experience here. So when guests finish their safari, they can come to a real East African marketplace and sit down and enjoy the authentic flavors of Africa.

If you savor the marketplace experience, you'll notice some incredible details, like bicycles and mopeds parked against the sides of buildings, a 1960s-era telephone pole with a mass of tangled wires, chairs tossed atop metal roofs, colorful tables and benches made to look like they're constructed of discarded wood planks, and clothing hanging from sagging rope lines.

And then there are the posters plastered on walls throughout the area. "The posters add layering," said Imagineer Emily O'Brien. And a touch of humor. One poster, advertising an herbalist, says the good doctor will "cure curses and evil spirits...all troubled marriages...all headaches...bad luck/bad debt." Some signs say, "Well-come. Very, very cold drinks."

O'Brien added:

> You really feel like you are actually in a real village in Africa. You have the whole gamut of experiences, with the central area, the theater district, specialty vendors, and a great market. Guests will really feel like they've been transported to another place for a really fun experience.

Opening Day Attractions in Africa

Highlights: Harambe, Kilimanjaro Safaris, Pangani Forest Exploration Trail, Wildlife Express to Conservation Station, Conservation Station

Dining: Tusker House, Kusafiri Coffee Shop and Bakery, Tamu Tamu Refreshments, African Lounge, Harambe Fruit Market

Shopping: Mombasa Marketplace/Ziwani Traders, Duke La Filimu, Out of the Wild

Current Attractions in Africa

Highlights: Festival of the Lion King, Harambe, Kilimanjaro Safaris, Gorilla Falls Exploration Trail, Rafiki's Planet Watch (which now includes Wildlife Express Train, Conservation Station and Affection Section)

Dining: Donald's Dining Safari at Tusker House, Kusafiri Coffee Shop and Bakery, Tamu Tamu Refreshments, Harambe Fruit Market, Harambe Market, Dawa Bar, Zuri's Sweets Shop

Shopping: Mombasa Marketplace

CHAPTER SEVEN

Conservation Station / Rafiki's Planet Watch

Outside the main building at Conservation Station—an area of the park located in the far reaches of Africa and only accessible by train—a huge montage of brightly colored animal and bird faces greeted opening-day guests. The animals seemed to be staring at the curious human visitors as they walked toward the entrance to the building. At that point, parents often stopped and asked their young children to identify as many of the animals pictured in the montage as they could. The excited responses included "a gorilla...an elephant...a lion...a wolf...a turtle." The families then proceeded inside, where they were greeted by the Hall of Animals, and hundreds more animals pictured on a large, curved mural, looking at each of every guest walking through the entryway. It was—and still is—a powerful message.

According to facility curator Dr. Jackie Ogden:

> The animals are looking *at* you and *to* you—the human species—for man represents both the greatest danger to the animals and their environment and their greatest hope for survival.

Conservation Station [today known as Rafiki's Planet Watch] is perhaps the most important section of Disney's Animal Kingdom. In a sense, Conservation Station embodied everything Animal Kingdom stands for and it demonstrates— in a clear, easy-to-understand educational platform—the park's true mission. Yes, there are thrilling experiences and exciting shows and adventures throughout the park. But at its core, Conservation Station hopes to inspire all those who visit to learn about animal care and, more importantly, be moved to take what they've learned and assume a more active role in conservation efforts upon returning home.

Conservation Station "is the real heart of the message at Animal Kingdom," said show writer Paula Kessler.

Zofia Kostyrko, part of the core team of Imagineers who first met in that "funky trailer" in the early 1990s to chart Animal Kingdom's course, was a key contributor to Conservation Station as lead designer. She brought a strong résumé of commercial design, as well as a love of children's art, to the table:

> Our show is for children and children-at-heart, to arouse their emotional feelings for animals by showing the beauty and richness of the animal kingdom. I started with master planning the park and then I worked on Safari Village and then the Asian safari, and when the Asian safari project was scrapped, I worked on Conservation Station. It brought together the conservation community and the Disney community. I worked very closely with Jackie Ogden, Ann Savage, and Beth Stevens.
>
> We reached out to the zoo community. We had Rick Barongi and Ray Mendez and the other people who were on the advisory board who came in. Jackie, Beth, and Ann Savage, the chief scientist, were there pretty early, most of the shape of [Conservation Station] was already set up, but they helped us adjust, refine, and fine-tune everything. Overall, we were very fortunate to work with the crème-de-la-crème of the zoo community. It's really satisfying to see how our shared work, in return, has changed zoo standards. [Animal Kingdom] was too big of a target to do it any other way than the right way. With Conservation Station, we hoped to set new standards for communicating and connecting with conservation issues.

Dr. Jackie Ogden brought a unique skillset to her position as the curator of Conservation Station. She began her career as a psychologist...for humans. After graduating from Western Washington University, she began taking courses in animal psychology. Her career path led her to several research-student positions at a variety of zoos. She earned her Ph.D. while at Zoo Atlanta, working closely with gorillas and other primates, studying both animal and human reaction to a variety of stimuli. In 1994, when San Diego Children's Zoo curator Rick Barongi left his post to join the Animal Kingdom planning team, his replacement was Dr. Ogden, who installed a number of innovative programs there.

With Barongi's urging, Ogden joined the Animal Kingdom team and began making contributions to Conservation Station. She said:

> We talk about problems and solutions for the many dangers faced by endangered animals around the world. [At Conservation Station,] we show everyone there are many things they can do, and inspire them to take part in supporting the welfare of animals and the world's environment.

The center piece of Conservation Station was a stage where presentations of rare or endangered animals took place every day. "Every demonstration will be different," Ogden said prior to the park's opening. Around the stage, wildlife and veterinary laboratories, interactive displays, and animal nurseries were within guests' views. On a giant map of the world, 11 areas were highlighted because that was where the world's most endangered animals could be found. Near this area were Animal Cams, interactive screens which showed photos and gave information on animals throughout the world.

In 1998, guests boarded the Wildlife Express steam train from an East Africa-inspired station in Harambe to Conservation Station. Along the way, they could see some of the backstage areas where many of the animals in the park were cared for. After stepping off the train following the 10-minute ride, guests walked a short distance through a lush woodland setting to the multi-faceted animal care facility. That train still makes its 1.2-mile trek many times during the day, chugging past those same state-of-the-art animal-care facilities.

The steam trains are a sight to behold for train buffs—they look as if they had been plucked right from the legendary Indian Peninsula Railroad. In fact, the engines and passenger cars were modeled after trains first built in 1898 at the

Horwich Locomotive Works in England. They ride on narrow-gauge rails, 3.3-feet wide, which is common for trains that traverse treacherous mountains and canyons. The Wildlife Express—actually, the train consists of five-cars that seat 250 guests in contoured seats facing sideways—was built in 1997 by Severn Lamb, Ltd., a noted model railroad company located in Alchester, England.

Joel Fritsche supervised the design and construction of the trains for Walt Disney Imagineering. He, in turn, coaxed veteran Disney trainmaker Bob Harpur out of retirement to assist with the project. Harpur helped locate and rebuild antique trains from Mexico for use in the Magic Kingdom and Fort Wilderness at Walt Disney World. Harpur and Fritsche, as well as former Imagineer Eddie Sotto, also had a big hand in the train design and installation at Disneyland Paris.

The Wildlife Express is themed to the Nth degree. Of course, on opening day, the trains looked as if they had been in service for decades. Their whistles were high-pitched, sharp, and distinctive; piled on top of each car were an assortment of boxes, crates, carpet bags, and wicker luggage. Passengers rode in open carriages, but were protected by waist-high shutters. The train has remained relatively unchanged over the past two decades, although with the expansion of Harambe, it now can be seen from a seating area as it chugs into and out of the Harambe station.

These days, the area is known as Rafiki's Planet Watch. Despite the name change, the facility remains true to its mission, offering a broad range of animal experiences, such as demonstrations, research programs, and a petting zoo. At the petting zoo, known as Affection Section, guests interact with a variety of rare, yet domesticated animals, all under the supervision of knowledgeable animal-care experts. In the Conservation Station section, guests can watch veterinarians caring for animals— everything from tooth extractions to vaccinations to actual surgeries.

Guests who view animal procedures and actual operations do so through a 15-foot wall of picture windows. The veterinarians working on the animals communicate with their interested audience by using an intercom pedal. Guests, in turn, are able to ask questions of the vets. The room itself is state of the art, with enough equipment to rival any major medical facility, animal or human.

As an added treat these days, young visitors to Rafiki's Planet Watch can interact with Disney Junior star Doc McStuffins, who has made a name for herself by caring for a different breed of animal...namely, the stuffed and stitched variety.

Opening Day Attractions in Conservation Station

Highlights: Wildlife Express Train, Affection Section, Conservation Station and the Hall of Animal Care, Interactive Exhibits

Dining: Munch Wagon

Shopping: Out of the Wild

Current Attractions in Rafiki's Planet Watch

Highlights: Wildlife Express Train, Affection Section, Conservation Station and the Hall of Animal Care, Interactive Exhibits

Dining: None

Shopping: None

CHAPTER EIGHT

DinoLand U.S.A.

In theory, DinoLand U.S.A. was nearly 70 million years in the making. The land, devoted to Earth's long-extinct "terrible lizards," opened with a relatively sparse collection of dino-themed attractions in 1998. The unquestioned centerpiece of DinoLand U.S.A. was Countdown to Extinction, a high-thrill attraction that took riders from Earth near the turn of the 21st century back to primeval days in a quest to save a dinosaur from extinction.

As guests approached the main entrance to DinoLand U.S.A. from a bridge that connected it to Safari Village, they were greeted by Dino-Sue, a replica of the largest Tyrannosaurus Rex ever found. The massive structure, which measured 40 feet in length and was 13 feet tall at the hip, was estimated to weigh 6–8 tons when it roamed the Earth. The original T-rex was unearthed in South Dakota in 1990; 90% of its skeleton was meticulously reassembled and has since been put on display at the Field Museum of Natural History in Chicago, Ill.

On either side of the entrance was an area that appealed to young paleontologists—the Boneyard. Here, youngsters could dig to their heart's content, searching for the skeletal remains of some of the world's mightiest creatures. On one side of the Boneyard was a playground where kids could run and climb. Then, after crossing over the Olden Gate Bridge, they found an excavation site that mimicked a real fossil park, a place where scientists conduct their "digs." After much digging of their own, kids would come across huge fossilized skeletons of a triceratops and a brontosaurus. The area was covered to shield from the sun and the "dirt" young paleontologists were digging was sand, so they wouldn't leave the area caked in mud.

Near the dig site was Restaurantosaurus, a cleverly themed and well-placed restaurant sponsored by McDonald's. The folks who gave us Big Macs also hosted DinoLand Snacks nearby.

Crustaceous Trail offered guests a glimpse at plants and animal species that have managed to survive since the days dinosaurs roamed the planet, things like cycads, ferns, and palms, as well as soft-shelled turtles and lizards.

Landscape architect Paul Comstock said:

> We were always, from early on, discussing how we would replicate these natural environments and animals from mythology or animals from the Jurassic period down to the current animals. What would the plants have been like then? What would the plants be like in each of those different eras? The dinosaur era, for instance, there are plants that were around during the age of dinosaurs that are still surviving today, as impossible as that might sound.

At the end of Crustaceous Trail, opening-day guests could visit the 1998 Dinosaur Jubilee, a temporary facility where dinosaur artifacts, including casts from real dinosaur skeletons, were on display. Not too far away was the Fossil Preparation Lab, where you could watch as paleontological experts prepared the original remains of the most complete T-rex skeleton ever found in the world. (Both displays were dismantled a few years later to make way for Chester and Hester's Dino-Rama.)

On opening day, Countdown to Extinction not only anchored DinoLand U.S.A., but was *the* major thrill ride in Animal Kingdom. Guests entered a building which housed a "once-secret research project of the Dino Institute, built as a discovery center and on-going research lab, dedicated to uncovering the mysteries of the past." The pre-show included a display of museum-quality murals, fossils, and dioramas that depicted how dinosaurs became extinct. Scientists concluded that a fiery meteor slammed into Earth 65 million years ago, causing a "nuclear winter" that wiped out the dinosaur population.

Guests were then ushered into a briefing room, where Institute Director Dr. Helen Marsh (played by actress Phylicia Rashad) greeted them:

I hope you enjoyed the quaint exhibits in the old wing. Today, that bare-bones approach is history. In a perfect blending of science and technology, the Dino Institute has created the Time Rover—an amazing vehicle that can literally transport you to the Age of Dinosaurs.

Dr. Marsh was joined by a paleontologist named Grant Seeker, who served as the guide for our journey back in time. But it quickly became apparent that Dr. Marsh and Seeker had different intentions: She was hoping to provide a thrilling, but peaceful excursion into prehistoric times, while he was set on using the Time Rover to find and return an imperiled iguanodon before it and its dino friends were wiped out by the asteroid-created "nuclear winter."

Guests then boarded the 12-passenger, all-terrain vehicle known as a Time Rover for their harrowing adventure back in time. The Time Rover, as well as the collection of frighteningly realistic-looking dinosaurs, were the stars of the attraction. The Time Rover ride concept was first used at Disneyland for the Indiana Jones and the Temple of the Forbidden Eye attraction, which opened in 1995. The Time Rover vehicle in Indiana Jones "is exactly the same as the dinosaur ride in Animal Kingdom," explained retired Imagineer Tony Baxter, with one notable exception: the presence of all those prehistoric creatures situated throughout the adventure. Joe Rohde devised the attraction's plot, while designing and serving as art director for the dinosaurs. Alec Scribner was the attraction's producer, and Paul Torrigino did artwork and overall scenic design.

The Time Rover is a complex, computer-guided Enhanced Motion Vehicle [EMV]. Once it's loaded with passengers and pulls out of the boarding area, it passes through a tunnel and hurtles back in time. During the trip, the vehicle bobs and weaves, stops and starts, and jerks side-to-side through an elaborately themed and lush primeval world populated by a host of prehistoric creatures. The dinosaurs, in fact, range from peaceful plant eaters to hungry and menacing carnivores.

The trip through time took a harrowing turn when a hail of small meteors struck the vehicle. What followed was a heart-pounding journey past menacing dinosaurs and the imminent threat of lightning, meteor showers, and ultimately, the "Big Bang." All the while, your vehicle was being chased by a cantankerous carnotaurus, the unquestioned villain of the attraction.

Show producer Ann Malmlund explained:

> We cast it the way we would cast a movie. You need a hero and you need a villain. In this case, our villain was an Audio-Animatronics tour-de-force.

In the end, the Time Rover narrowly escapes the harrowing nuclear winter, the iguanodon is saved, and your vehicle returns safely home.

The carnotaurus—and indeed, all of the prehistoric creatures on display in Countdown to Extinction—follow in a long line of Disney dinos. There were dinosaurs on display in the Ford's Magic Skyway attraction at the 1964–1965 New York World's Fair (which, after the fair closed, took up residence along the Disneyland Railroad route) and a menacing collection of giants populated Ellen's Energy Adventure in the Universe of Energy pavilion at Epcot. And then there's the playful-looking dino named Gertie stationed at Echo Lake in Disney's Hollywood Studios.

When Disney released the animated film *Dinosaur* in 2000, it seemed logical that executives would try to tie the movie to the Animal Kingdom attraction. So, around the time of the film's release, the name of the attraction was changed to DINOSAUR, and the name Countdown to Extinction became...well, extinct.

In 2002, DinoLand U.S.A. received a major upgrade with the introduction of Chester and Hester's Dino-Rama, an area of the park that gave the Imagineers an excuse to display their tongue-in-cheek humor. Clever signs are everywhere, like "Going into extinction. Everything must go." The area looks as if it had been inspired by a church bazaar or a Midwestern roadside carnival...or both. The remnants of painted parking lot lines can be seen in the pavement and the buildings look as if they were thrown together without much rhyme or reason. There's even the occasional manhole cover.

Joe Rohde said:

> To create a convincing abandoned parking lot for people who see parking lots every day? That's actually really

hard. This surface is so convincing that it is ignored completely. But there is no way this surface could stand up to the traffic it receives on a hot summer day if it were actually asphalt. It is sculpture.

Chester and Hester's Dino-Rama also is a fun and light-hearted place that's geared to the young...and the young at heart.

Rohde explained the genesis of Dino-Rama:

As a boy, I used to love road trips. Once we moved to California from Hawaii, we would regularly take off on drives across the West, sometimes totally spontaneously. We'd be headed from Van Nuys to Big Bear and my dad would announce, "Let's go visit my sister in Ely, Nevada!" And off we'd go [check a map for how crazy this is]. He abhorred chains [motels], so we would eat, sleep, and shop with whatever meager funds we had "where the locals go."

Old roadside America was so weird it was beyond a question of tastefulness or kitsch. It was actual, independent personality, expressed without a fleck of concern for what someone else might think. That's what this is. [Chester and Hester's] is for kids who haven't yet learned what's tasteful, elegant, cool, or trendy. Joyous excess. Not for everyone, but I sort of grin every time I see it and remember my days poking through trays of arrowheads and fossil shark teeth, and posing with plaster dinos.

When you enter Dino-Rama, you're greeted by a giant, but whimsical and seemingly inflated dinosaur which stands about 50-feet tall. At the entrance are smaller dino creatures that are decidedly more fun than ferocious. There are two main attractions within Dino-Rama's confines: Primeval Whirl and TriceraTop Spin, which are family-friendly, carnival-based rides.

TriceraTop Spin follows in the classic spinning ride tradition of Dumbo, the Magic Carpets of Aladdin, and Astro Orbiter in the Magic Kingdom in that you climb into a themed ride vehicle (in this case, a friendly infant dinosaur) and spin round and round while raising and lowering your dino to enhance the experience. Primeval Whirl, on the other hand, takes spinning to new heights. It's a roller-coaster-type attraction that sees your vehicle go up, down, round and round, with several heart-pounding, whip-like turns thrown in to make the experience quite exhilarating.

Opening Day Attractions in DinoLand U.S.A.

Highlights: Countdown to Extinction, Boneyard, Cretaceous Trail, 1998 Dinosaur Jubilee, Fossil Preparation Lab

Dining: Restaurantosaurus, Dino Diner, DinoLand Snacks

Shopping: None

Current Attractions in DinoLand U.S.A.

Highlights: DINOSAUR, Boneyard, Fossil Fun Games, Primeval Whirl, TriceraTop Spin

Dining: Restaurantosaurus, Dino Diner, Trilo-Bites, Dino-Bite Snacks

Shopping: Chester & Hester's Dinosaur Treasures, Dino Institute Shop

CHAPTER NINE

Asia

It has happened to every Disney theme park since the opening of Disneyland in 1955: at some point, guests grow weary of the attractions in the park and want—*demand*—more thrill rides. When Animal Kingdom opened, there was Countdown to Extinction in DinoLand U.S.A. and not much else when it came to raising the thrill meter. The Asia section of the park, which was still under construction when the park opened in 1998, seemed to be the logical choice for the placement of future white-knuckle adventures.

On opening day, only the Flights of Wonder attraction at the Caravan Stage and a Discovery River Boat dock, called Upcountry Landing, were up and running in Asia. "Additional Asia adventures will open in early 1999," proclaimed the opening-day guide maps. For all intents and purposes, Asia on opening day wasn't so much a land as it was a large construction site brimming with potential.

Flights of Wonder was a pleasant respite, but hardly fell under the umbrella of a thrilling attraction. The show took place in an outdoor theater, overlooking Discovery River, and seated 1,250 guests. The stage set replicated the walls of a fortified, if weather-beaten town in Asia, with cubby hole-like insets that provided a natural "home" for the birds in the show as they awaited their cues to take flight. The stars of Flights of Wonder—falcons, macaws, vultures, owls, toucans, and hawks—flew around (and sometimes right over) the audience, demonstrating a variety of avian behaviors under the care and watchful eyes of skilled trainers.

A year after opening, the Discovery River boats were shut down and the Upcountry Landing became a covered photo-op area. But as promised in the park brochure, Asia opened two new attractions in 1999: Maharajah Jungle Trek and Kali River Rapids (originally called Tiger Rapids Run). Jungle Trek, a walkthrough similar to Gorilla Falls Exploration trail in Africa, allowed Disney's planners to display animals indigenous to Asia, among them Bengal tigers, Komodo dragons, and gibbons. A Bengal tiger viewing area was built, allowing guests to get within inches (behind a glass enclosure, of course) of the beautiful big cats as they romped around on a grassy hillside or amid "ancient" ruins. It was not unusual to see the tigers splashing in water playing mischievously with a large ball or jumping up and down from tree limbs, looking every bit like their distant feline cousins, the average house cat.

In addition to the tigers, dragons, and gibbons, also seen along the Jungle trek were bats, blackbucks, Eids deer, banteng, and Malayan tapir. There was a strong conservationist tone to the area, which touted the trek as "a walking tour through the royal forest of Anandapur." A park brochure read:

All the creatures you see depend on the forest for survival. As more trees are cut for human use, less and less space remains for wildlife. Preserving this forest provides jobs for the people of Anandapur and encourages the local villagers to become guardians of wildlife. Our ancient traditions are centered on compassion for all living things, with a belief in the Earth as the common heritage and responsibility of all. We are pleased you have visited the Royal Forest and hope you will consider ways that you and your village can help preserve natural habitats at home and around the world. Every concerned person is a foundation stone for our wildlife's future.

Kali River Rapids gave Animal Kingdom another thrill ride, one that also let overheated guests cool off while shooting the rapids and dodging waterfalls as their six-passenger rubber raft careened down a raging river. Near the raft's final, treacherous plunge, raft riders witness a rain-soaked forest of fire-blackened trees, some still smoldering. It's a subtle, yet effective way to demonstrate how clear-cutting a forest opens the suddenly bare land to devastating erosion. Of course, when the raft takes the plunge, guests tend to turn their attention to another matter: how to dry off after getting a thorough soaking.

Perhaps the most impressive aspect of Kali River Rapids is the queue area *before* you board your raft. Along the queue, guests pass through the Kali Tiger Temple, one of the most elaborately themed areas in a park that oozes with elaborate theming. There's a covered courtyard with a cobra fountain and sculptures and many interesting drawings above before you enter the temple. Here, a prayer wheel, brass gongs, and Balinese puppets are on display, as is a case filled with live geckos. Inspiration for the queue was taken from Imagineers' visits to Nepal, Java, and Thailand.

Even with the additions of Maharajah Jungle Trek and Kali River Rapids, the Asia section of the park was destined for bigger and better thrills.

In 2006, Animal Kingdom debuted what, at the time, was its signature thrill ride, a roller-coaster disguised as a freight train that hurtles guests around and through a stunning replica of Mount Everest. Expedition Everest, which at nearly 200 feet tall can be seen from nearly any location in the park, combines key elements of three classic Disney attractions: Big Thunder Mountain (a runaway train), Maelstrom, the now-closed boat ride in Epcot's Norway pavilion (a portion of the ride goes backwards), and the Matterhorn Bobsleds in Disneyland (a legendary, snow-capped mountain with a menacing furry creature on the loose in the bowels of the attraction).

What sets Expedition Everest apart from most other theme park attractions is its exquisite attention to detail.

As with the park itself, Animal Kingdom mastermind Joe Rohde put together a team of Imagineers who hit the road to do extensive research, spending considerable time in the Himalayan region of Asia, gathering information not only about Mount Everest, but also the people who inhabit the region and—lest we forget—the mysterious Yeti, who, legend has it, ferociously protects Everest from intruders.

Jay Rasulo, then chairman of Disney Parks and Resorts, said:

> This extraordinary expedition...is another example of the lengths to which Walt Disney Imagineering will go to research subject matter in developing our storylines.

Added Rohde:

> We are going to incredible lengths to tell this story,
> [researching] cultural and spiritual legends through
> local people who have reported sightings of the Yeti, and
> governments who preserve pristine lands in the name
> of the creature known as "protector of the mountains."

In 1991, Rohde did a rendering of a mountain to be placed
in the confines of Asia, but "it was a mountain in Bhutan, not
Nepal," he said. He rolled it up and placed it in a box, but didn't
forget about it:

> When the challenge [of building an attraction themed
> to a mountain] came back, I remembered I had that ren-
> dering. It's one of the best examples of how real art is in
> Animal Kingdom.

Expedition Everest also is an example of what Rohde calls
"the intrinsic value of nature." In Tibetan culture, "the Yeti is
a very real presence...he is the protector and the defender of
the untouched virgin, ancient forest."

For guests, the Expedition Everest experience begins as
you enter the imaginary, yet stunningly realistic village
known as Serka Zong. From here, Rohde explains, the drama
builds exponentially:

> The Himalayan culture is full of ritualized architecture,
> encouraging great harmony and structure. The colors of
> the village, the carved animal heads on the doors, the
> totems—it's all very symbolic and authentic.

Rohde's team brought back more than 8,000 props from
their travels, many museum quality and many put on display
in the buildings of Serka Zong and along the attraction's
queue. "Why do we put in this detail when guests aren't neces-
sarily going to see it?" Rohde said, answering a question with
a question. As any Imagineer worth his weight in FastPasses
will tell you, guests *absorb* those details.

The buildings in the village, as you might expect, look as if
they're centuries old. The stonework appears off-kilter, sagging
and distorted, as if one side slowly settled into the ground and
the other side remained upright and rigid. The wood elements
of the structures were weathered by using hammers, chain

saws, and blowtorches. Adorning the buildings are colorful flags, inspired by Himalayan prayer flags which are believed to send thoughts and prayers into the wind as they flutter. In addition, several totems dot the landscape, as does a three-story temple. The buildings are realistic representations of what you might expect to find in the foothills on your way to Mount Everest: there's the Shangri-la Trekkers Inn and Internet Café, as well as the "recently opened" Yeti Palace Hotel.

After traveling through the village (which cleverly disguises the FastPass and standby queues for the attraction), you come upon a booking office to obtain permits for your journey and a general store (Gupta's Gear) to purchase supplies. There is a stunning collection of artifacts of Tibetan culture...and some not-so-subtle reminders about the Yeti. Posters depict terrifying encounters with the dreaded abominable snowman and there are even some crushed and crumpled pieces of metal, further supporting the creature's existence and its ferocity. A museum (formerly a tea house) devoted to the Yeti sports a collection of paintings, maps, photos, and artifacts. At the end of the museum, there's a warning to all those who still have the courage to proceed:

> You are about to enter the sacred domain of the Yeti, guardian and protector of the Forbidden Mountain. Those who proceed with respect and reverence for the sanctity of the natural environment and its creatures should have no fear. To all others—a warning—you risk the wrath of the Yeti.

Rohde said:

> By the time you leave the museum, you're hopefully convinced that the Yeti is real.

At long last, explorers reach the bustling train station and are loaded onto the Anandapur Rail Service, an "aging" 34-passenger former tea plantation train for the trek to the Forbidden Mountain. As guests climb aboard, steam comes belching from the train's underbelly and its smokestack. The train, although appearing to be weather-beaten and aged, is constructed of sturdy aluminum and fiberglass; the seats are cushioned and comfortable, with lap bars keeping riders secure.

The excursion begins innocently enough, slowly winding through lush, green countryside at the base of the mountain before climbing up a rickety-looking bridge. The train passes through a majestic shrine, honoring the Yeti, before chugging up Mount Everest itself. During the ascent, one sound is noticeably missing: new design techniques were employed so that the click-click-click usually associated with a roller coaster making an upward climb into the mountain's peaks have been eliminated.

The Disney-created Mount Everest is a technological marvel. Much like the Matterhorn Bobsleds attraction in Disneyland, Expedition Everest is a roller-coaster that weaves its way in and out of a mountain, with a mythical, yet terrifying creature waiting to wreak havoc inside. Unlike the Matterhorn, which was designed by Imagineer Bob Gurr by using just drafting tools, slide rulers, and good ol' common sense, the Imagineers employed computer technology to craft Animal Kingdom's perilous peak, cutting design time from about three years to 18 months.

To achieve the authenticity he wanted, Rohde took a small team to the source—the real Mount Everest, the world's tallest mountain located between Nepal, Tibet, and China:

> I have always believed in taking the Imagineers to real places to have real experiences.

When they returned from their fact-finding excursion, the artists—armed with photos, drawings, and unforgettable images in their minds—began making clay versions of the Forbidden Mountain. Once they settled on the design they felt best embodied Mount Everest, the arduous task of making a 20-story-tall mountain on top of a flat, dirt field began. Heavy steel beams—some rigid to support the structure of the mountain, others more giving to handle the weight of the ride's track and the coaster trains that would rumble on it— were set in place. Rather than use traditional scaffolding on the outside, the Imagineers employed a system of tab arms, which looked like toothpicks sticking out of the sides of the mountain. Workers would place wood planks on top of the arms and then place the "skin" of the mountain onto the inner support beams. The workers affixed six-foot-square pieces of rebar, called chips, to the sides of the mountain, much like a massive, 3D jigsaw puzzle.

In all, 38 miles of rebar was used to construct the outer layer of the mountain, with 32,000 bags of cement covering the rebar. Before the cement dried, large sheets of aluminum foil were pressed onto it to give the mountain sides a jagged, realistic texture. Finally, 2,000 gallons of paint in different shades were used, including four shades to replicate snow.

The coaster track also was a big challenge for the designers, simply because halfway through the attraction, the train stops and reverses course, heading backwards. To accomplish that, an elaborate track switch system was devised. After several dips and turns and a passage through a tunnel, the train is forced to a screeching halt when the track up ahead is gnarled and impassable. Apparently, forces beyond our understanding are at work here. Could it be the Yeti? For six seconds, the train sits still as anxiety levels climb among the guests on board.

Suddenly, the train is set in motion again—but this time, backwards, leaving the mangled track behind, all the while building speed while heading full-tilt into the darkened unknown. Thanks to the track switch system, the train glides onto another section of track and enters the mountain. It dips downward and then climbs sharply, with shadows, silhouetted projections, and noticeable climate changes enhancing the experience. Just as suddenly, the train grinds to another halt, this time with the back end of the train noticeably more elevated on the track than the front. Right after a projection of the Yeti flashes across an inner mountain wall, the train lurches forward again. The track-switching device guides the train to the left and outside the mountain, dropping 80 gut-wrenching feet in the process before whooshing through a series of high-speed twists and turns. Before reaching the station and safety, though, the train careens past the harrowing figure of the Yeti.

When the attraction opened, Rohde said:

> Seeing the Yeti really startles guests because it is so real, so convincing. Nothing this big or this fast has ever been created. The Yeti is embedded in Tibetan culture and he's justifiably angry [to see intruders].

Nineteen functions were built into the figure to provide motion, using 3,000 psi of hydraulic thrust to achieve those realistic movements. When the ride was first introduced, the Yeti would raise his right paw and lunge toward the train as it zipped past. But technical issues have reduced the legendary creature to a more passive, though still menacing, stance as the train swooshes by.

Expedition Everest was the thrill ride that Animal Kingdom guests had been yearning for since opening day. The lines were long in the weeks following its opening in the spring of 2006 and they've stayed long ever since. During the opening-night celebration for the new attraction, Rohde—playing the role of a proud father—took Peter Hillary on a personal guided tour of the attraction's elaborate queue before joining him for a spin on the coaster. Peter Hillary is the son of Sir Edmund Hillary, who, in 1953, joined Sherpa mountaineer Tenzing Norgay to become the first people to successfully climb Mount Everest. In 2002, Peter Hillary and Norgay's son climbed Everest together to celebrate the 50th anniversary of their fathers' accomplishment.

In the shadows of Expedition Everest is the one attraction in Animal Kingdom that's always been out of place: Theater in the Wild. Guide maps since opening day have listed it as a part of DinoLand U.S.A., although the theming of the early shows staged under its roof were more conducive to Africa or nearby Asia. When the park opened, Theater in the Wild was home to the Journey into Jungle Book stage show—hardly the kind of setting you'd expect to see in the Cretaceous period. The theater, which seated 1,500 guests, had a roof, but was not enclosed, meaning heat and humidity made conditions quite uncomfortable for guests and performers most of the year.

Journey into Jungle Book, based on the endearing work by Rudyard Kipling, was billed as an "hilarious and unusual stage production," employing a "new breed of 'humanimals' (highly mobile costumed characters combining human performers and innovative puppetry). Many of the most popular songs from Disney's animated classic *The Jungle Book* were performed by "humanimal" re-creations of Mowgli, Baloo, Kaa, King Louie, Shere Kahn, and Colonel Hathi.

By the year 2000, the show had been changed, although the jungle theme remained intact. Journey into Jungle Book was supplanted by Tarzan Rocks! The new show was louder and more energetic, with amplified guitars and acrobatic performers on skates darting across the stage. As a guide map from 2000 read:

> Swing your way into this high-energy rock concert featuring Tarzan, Jane, Terk, and a cast of jungle gymnasts.

As part of the expansion to the area, a bridge was erected linking Asia to DinoLand U.S.A., making Theater in the Wild more accessible.

In 2006, in conjunction with the opening of Expedition Everest, Disney pulled the plug on Tarzan Rocks! and opted for a complete remake of both the show and the venue. Theater in the Wild was refurbished and enclosed, allowing for guest-friendly amenities like air conditioning. Production capabilities also were enhanced, with increased lighting and better sound reproduction, enabling Disney's creative staff to craft a Broadway-style show. When Finding Nemo: The Musical debuted in late 2006, it was hailed as a creative masterpiece and became an instant success...and a quantum leap over its predecessors.

Walt Disney Creative Entertainment developed the new show, which featured talented performers who sang, danced, and controlled puppets in the shapes of the main characters from the hit movie Finding Nemo. The colorful, wildly imaginative production also featured acrobats and animated backdrops to create a believable undersea world. Several new songs, written by award-winning Broadway veterans Bobby Lopez and Kristen Anderson-Lopez, enhanced the production. Among the original performers in Finding Nemo: The Musical was actress Vanessa Ray, who stars in the CBS-TV drama Blue Bloods. Ray, who originated the lead role of Nemo, called her eight months at Animal Kingdom "really special—it was the first time I created a role and I met some of the best friends of my life." Fans of the Disney TV series Pretty Little Liars also will remember Ray for her role as CeCe Drake.

Despite the changes, Theater in the Wild remains an anomaly. It doesn't fit in with the prehistoric theming of

DinoLand U.S.A., while Finding Nemo: The Musical is based on creatures from the ocean and has very little to do with Asia. Although Theater in the Wild fits in well with Animal Kingdom's mission, it is a stand-alone attraction with no ties to a specific land in the park, guide maps to the contrary.

Opening Day Attractions in Asia

Highlights: Flights of Wonder, Discovery River Boats at Upcountry Landing

Dining: None

Shopping: None

Current Attractions in Asia

Highlights: Flights of Wonder, Maharajah Jungle Trek, Kali River Rapids, Expedition Everest, Rivers of Light

Dining: Caravan Road, Mr. Kamel's, Warung Outpost, Drinkwallah, Yak & Yeti Restaurant, Yak & Yeti Local Food Cafes, Yak & Yeti Quality Beverages, Anandapur Ice Cream Truck, Thirsty River Bar & Trek Snacks

Shopping: Serka Zong Bazaar

CHAPTER TEN

Camp Minnie-Mickey

When Animal Kingdom opened in 1998, park guests had a broad range of experiences to choose from, including a safari through an African savannah; the creepy, crawly world of bugs; and traveling back in time to the age of dinosaurs. Exciting stuff. And then there was Camp Minnie-Mickey which, save for its lone major attraction, a stage show called Festival of the Lion King, and a Pocahontas-themed children's show, was little more than a grand and glorious photo-op area.

During the planning stages for the park, Camp Minnie-Mickey wasn't even on the designers' radar; a land about mythical creatures was. In keeping with the park's theme of celebrating animals, be they living, extinct, or mythical, this land—known as either Mythia or Beastly Kingdom in the early mock-ups—was to explore the fantastic world of animals of lore, storybook creatures such as unicorns and dragons. In fact, close study of Animal Kingdom's opening-day logo shows a small parade of animals, including a lion, an elephant, a dinosaur, and a winged dragon, all marching in front of a stylized Tree of Life.

However, a land devoted to mythical creatures never gained much traction, at least not during the years before the park opened.

Marty Sklar said:

> It just didn't catch on. One of the reasons for that, at the time, was there wasn't a lot of money to spend on that area, because we were still trying to develop the rest of the park as best as we could. Until recently, Animal Kingdom was only a daytime park, so you had different dynamics. I think Joe [Rohde] never lost that idea of making the area a mythical area. He was pretty fixed on

it from the beginning, making it a contrast to the rest of the park. "

(Rohde would get that contrast—and then some—with the opening of Pandora in 2017.)

In the end, the land for mythical creatures was scrapped. In its place went Camp Minnie-Mickey, themed after a summer vacation retreat reminiscent of camps in the Adirondack Mountains in upstate New York. You know: hiking, fishing, campfires and s'mores. The idea was to show the place where everyone's favorite Disney characters went on vacation (after "working" in the theme parks).

The characters, dressed in khaki safari garb, with some wearing faux pith helmets, were featured throughout Camp Minnie-Mickey. There were four huts in the camp where guests could say "'cheese" and pose for photos with Mickey, Minnie, and Goofy, as well as some of the characters from *The Jungle Book* and *The Lion King*. It was an area clearly geared to young children. Thankfully, it was well shaded under mature cedar and birch trees.

Children—as well as a powerful message about conservation—were the impetus for the Pocahontas and Her Forest Friends show in Camp Minnie-Mickey. The 12-minute presentation was held several times a day in a 350-seat mini-arena called Grandmother Willow's Grove.

The theme of the live show was to discover which animal could best protect America's forests and the creatures who live in them from destruction. Grandmother Willow, whose face was embedded in a tree trunk, was the show's host. Pocahontas, along with a variety of her animal friends, tried to help the wise grand dame in finding that one special forest protector. "You must ask the animals," Grandmother Willow said, and Pocahontas set out to do just that.

There followed a parade of Pocahontas' animal friends onto the stage—from an armadillo to a turtle to rabbits and a skunk...even a prickly porcupine—as guests learned about each animal's strengths and weaknesses when it came to their ability to protect the forest. The message, however was that the animal best suited to save the forests was none other than man himself. It was a classic example of Disney "edu-tainment"...an entertaining show with a strong message. Still, while enjoyable, it wasn't what you'd call an E-ticket attraction.

By far the most popular attraction in Camp Minnie-Mickey was Festival of the Lion King, which was staged in a rustic, open-air amphitheater resembling an Adirondack summer theater. The venue seated 1,000 guests who, even in the last few rows, were extremely close to the action. (After several years of guests and performers sweltering during the show, the theater was enclosed and air-conditioned.)

Initial reviews of *The Lion King*-themed show tossed around words like "spectacle," "celebration," and "pageantry." The show was that...and much more. The seating area was divided into four sections. The guests seated in each section were labeled lion, giraffe, warthog, and elephant, and they took part in a lively pre-show where they were asked to replicate the sounds made by their designated animal. There were four tracks embedded in the ground, dividing each section, with all leading from backstage areas to center stage. On these tracks, four giant rolling stages moved in toward the center of the arena during the opening segment of the show.

The star of the show, Simba, rolled in on one of the stages, which replicated Pride Rock from the movie. The animated lion cub stood 12 feet tall. Another stage rolled out, featuring a playful elephant and a waterfall, while the other stages were highlighted by two swaying giraffe heads, and a jungle mesa with *Lion King* stars Timon and Pumbaa propped on top. Singers, dressed in colorful African tribal costumes, opened the show with a rousing rendition of "I Just Can't Wait to Be King." The level of energy was ramped up exponentially when a group known as the Tumble Monkeys made their appearance. The colorfully clad "primates" were, in reality, world-class gymnasts in disguise. With "Hakuna Matata" blasting over the loudspeakers, the monkeys bounced playfully on trampolines and swung from ropes.

Other highlights included tribal warriors on stilts during a performance of "Be Prepared," as well as giant bird-like devices and aerialists. The rousing finale included stirring renditions of "The Lion Sleeps Tonight" and "The Circle of Life." Many of the performers in Festival of the Lion King either had

Broadway credits on their résumés or used their experience in the show as a springboard to the Great White Way.

When Disney's creative minds were tasked with designing a new land based on the mega-hit movie *Avatar*, Camp Minnie-Mickey seemed like the logical place to put it. Since the land was originally intended to house mythical creatures such as dragons and unicorns, the placement of the Na'vi from Pandora in the area was fitting. To make way for the land, Pocahontas and Her Forest Friends was scrapped, as were the photo huts, but the Festival of the Lion King show was just too popular to close down.

So, a new venue was built on an available tract of land in Africa, behind Tusker House, in the expanded Harambe Village, giving Festival of the Lion King a setting perfectly suited to its Africa-themed storyline.

Opening Day Attractions in Camp Minnie-Mickey

Highlights: Character greeting areas, Festival of the Lion King, Grandmother Willow's Grove

Dining: Chip 'n' Dale's Cookie Cabin, Funnel Cake Cart

Shopping: None

CHAPTER ELEVEN

Animal Kingdom Attractions Never Built

Deep in the heart of Asia, on the shores of Discovery River, a small peninsula juts out into the waterway. Its positioning makes it a perfect place to snap a photo of the imposing Expedition Everest looming in the distance. On this spit of land, the Imagineers placed a small temple, which lends itself well to the exotic nature of the Nepalese-inspired town of Serka Zong that sits at the base of Mount Everest.

Unbeknownst to most people who visit the area is that tucked inside the temple lies a hidden treasure—a time capsule. Inside the capsule are items placed by members of the original Animal Kingdom design team. Among these items are sketches and drawings made by the Imagineers of proposed—but never realized—attractions for the park.

Zofia Kostyrko explained:

> We all put stuff in the time capsule. I put drawings of multiple attractions that didn't happen. I don't know when the capsule is supposed to be opened, but there are some amazing things that everybody on the team put in there.

Ms. Kostyrko, who was the original designer of the Asia section of the park before she left the company to raise her two young daughters, had one concept that never saw the light of day, but may well have served as the inspiration for the current Rivers of Light show:

> One of the ideas I had was this beautiful, electric show on the lake near where Expedition Everest is now. As you well know, Disney has a morgue of ideas. I haven't seen

the Rivers of Light show, but maybe it's close to one of the ideas I had. It just shows that no good idea ever goes away.

During the first few months of the park's operation, a precursor to the Rivers of Light show was featured as several large animals on rafts could be seen from the shoreline.

In the years leading up to Animal Kingdom's opening, Ms. Kostryko said, the ideas being tossed around for possible attractions were numerous:

> We'd be locked up for the whole day in that trailer, coming up with different realms of ideas. There were many concepts that didn't make it.

Paul Comstock, the park's principal landscape architect, added:

> Those early meetings were really great. Basically, you have a table of contents, like a book. There would be a chapter, which would be the big idea, like the African safari. Then we would sit around with 3x5 cards and you'd say, "There could be lions looking out over animals that they prey on." We would generate all these different ideas. After you'd look at some ideas for an hour or two, you'd say that's not really a good idea, so it would go into the dumper or a file cabinet. The team often was in those meetings to create a palette of ideas that would visually support what each attraction would be.
>
> The ringleader of that was Joe [Rohde]; he was the team captain. He'd write everything down on a 3x5 card and stick it up on the wall. Those ideas would be generated for everything. Sometimes there would be 20 or 30 index cards under one idea of a certain habitat or area and how that could potentially work. The team often was in those meetings to create ideas that would visually support what each attraction would be. There would be a painting and below it there would be samples...like Joe's classic drawing of ride vehicles driving through a herd of giraffes and there are grasses and acacia trees in the background and I would then support that with different types of materials.

When the team was overflowing with ideas, Comstock said, "the big guns"—Disney's top executives—would be called in:

> Marty Sklar would call up Frank Wells and Michael Eisner to set up a meeting, and we'd show them all this artwork of upwards of 20 different potential attractions. We'd run it by these guys and say, "What do you think about ideas A, B or C?" And they'd say, "We'd don't like A or B, but C is really great. And that other one's a good idea, too."

The ideas that made it through this arduous process became park attractions. The ones that didn't? They became the stuff of Disney parks lore.

Ms. Kostryko gave an example:

> We had a concept for a giant carousel, a huge flying, leaping, swinging thing with all kinds of animals, becoming the center of the park instead of the Tree of Life.

Before the It's Tough to Be a Bug show took up residence in the base of the Tree of Life, early plans called for a restaurant to be sited in the tree's root base. It would have been known as the Roots Restaurant. Additionally, ideas were floated which would have allowed guests to climb up the Tree of Life, similar to the Swiss Family Robinson experience in the Magic Kingdom.

Ms. Kostryko said:

> There was an idea for a land we originally called Mythia, where we were going to have Kraken the monster and a unicorn maze and a dragon. That land, which for a time also became known as Beastly Kingdom, was to be placed in the area once occupied by Camp Minnie-Mickey. It was clearly an effort to fulfill Animal Kingdom's mission of being about animals—living, extinct, and mythical.
>
> There were a whole bunch of ideas that we tossed around. One of them we played with when Jim Henson was still alive. For a brief time, we were looking at including the Muppets in a Jim Henson section of the park dedicated to younger audiences. I still have napkin sketches I did of Missy Piggy and Kermit the Frog in gas masks going through a very polluted river. It was

a combination of *Nightmare Before Christmas* and the Muppets at Animal Kingdom.

In her role as the original lead designer of Asia, Ms. Kostyrko proposed several concepts for the land that didn't make the cut:

The one big thing that didn't make it in Asia was a safari, but that eventually became Kali River Rapids.

The Asian safari was supposed to be equal in size to the African safari and it was going to be a boat journey from the Himalayas all the way down to Indonesia and then all the way back through India. The journey would tell the story of the people and their varied, continually evolving relationship with nature—it was very conservationist in spirit. After talking about how in India, some people are clear-cutting the forests, while others are living on the edge of the recovering forests, you'd go to the extremely diverse, rugged jungles of Borneo and you'd have total wilderness.

We were going to have Asian elephants in that enclosure walking above us on the bridges over the river. There was going to be a phenomenal restaurant designed by [former Imagineer] Kim Minichiello, one of the best themed dining spaces I've ever see. Kim took all the different parts of Indian cultural traditions and fitted them together like a perfect Rubik's Cube; it was going to be an amazingly complex, seamless flowing space. Each room was going to have different theming...absolutely beautiful. Then, an Asian nature walk was designed in the middle of the safari river loop, a little bit like in Africa. We were going to have a flooded village inside of it. Again, the whole concept was built around the question of man's interests versus nature's interests and how do you balance the two to sustain both, as they indeed are one in the same.

Whether a proposed attraction ultimately made it to the park or ended up in a time capsule, one design concept remained constant: conservation.

Ms. Kostyryko said:

We were always very aware and conscious of making sure that whatever we designed and built in Asia and Africa had a really strong conservationist's core to tell the story. The push and pull between people's needs and environment and animals' needs is never a simple black-and-white, good-versus-evil story. We took the lead from the Bronx Zoo's Conservation Society, where they had these exhibits that showed both sides of the coin. It's a really, really complex issue, never black and white.

CHAPTER TWELVE

Animal Kingdom Lodge

About a five-minute drive from the entrance of Animal Kingdom sits one of the most creative, innovative, and breathtakingly beautiful resorts in all of Walt Disney World. It's called Disney's Animal Kingdom Lodge (AKL) and it's the perfect complement to Animal Kingdom theme park.

Walt Disney World's on-property resorts have a reputation for top-shelf service and impeccable accommodations. But what makes each of them unique is they all tell a story. Indeed, theming is what makes each resort on WDW property stand out from most other resorts. Want to experience the easy-going way of life in the Conch Republic? Try staying at Disney's Old Key West Resort. Want a resort with a South Pacific island flare? Stop by Disney's Polynesian Village. In the mood for a Pacific Northwest log cabin experience, complete with a cozy fireplace? There's Disney's Wilderness Lodge.

When Disney gave the green light for a new resort adjacent to Animal Kingdom, it was with the intent of making it an extension of the Animal Kingdom story. At Animal Kingdom Lodge, that story centers around African culture and the animals so important to it. AKL is a celebration of the joy and pride of Africa's rich history and traditions. In announcing the new resort—interestingly, during the opening of Animal Kingdom park on April 22, 1998—then-Walt Disney World president Al Weiss said:

> We're building a whole new savannah. We had to raise the hotel up one level so the animals can wander underneath.

Animal Kingdom Lodge opened in 2001, three years after the park. It was an immediate hit. During opening-day ceremonies, Roy E. Disney said:

They [meaning his father, Roy O. Disney, and his uncle Walt] would have been thrilled with what has been created here and would have thought it a wonderfully appropriate addition to their company.

The most endearing aspect of the resort, its savannahs, total 46 acres. The three massive animal enclosures—Sunset, Arusha, and Uzima—give guests the distinct feeling that they had been transported to the heart of deepest, darkest Africa. "Even though Animal Kingdom Lodge is a hotel, for us it's a show scene," Joe Rohde said. The resort's thatched roofs, he added, "establish a sense of actually being in Africa."

Paul Comstock, Animal Kingdom's principal landscape architect, also was responsible for the landscaping at AKL, which went a long way in establishing the resort's authentic characteristics.

He said:

[Animal Kingdom Lodge] was developed by a group of people, headed by [former Imagineer] Wing Chao, who built all the hotels that surrounded the parks. What they did was hire an Orlando firm to produce the drawings for the lodge. What Wing said to the developer was, "I'm going to send Paul to your office and he's going to design all that." I spent two weeks in the developer's office and I designed the landscape for the lodge.

The thinking behind the placement of the savannahs around the lodge was to present an experience for guests that replicated a safari adventure through the Serengeti in Africa. With that in mind, Comstock said:

We used the same palette of plant material that we had generated for the Animal Kingdom theme park. By the time we built the hotel, we had experimented with and had planted 375 different species of grasses alone. What we were looking for was a holy grail of grass plants that the animals did not like to eat. We knew the grasses that they would eat, but we were looking for the grasses that we could put out there, that people could drive through and it would look like the grassy savannah area. Ultimately, we found about 10 different kinds of grasses.

Comstock took his boots-on-the-ground mindset and applied it to his work on Animal Kingdom Lodge:

> Everyone wanted to work inside, in an air-conditioned office, with their computers and everything. I went to Joe and said I wanted to put a tent out in the savannah so I could monitor and guide the team as it built this thing. I wanted to be actually inside the landscape.

First-time guests at Animal Kingdom Lodge felt a sense of amazement as they walked the grounds. As they approached the main lobby from the parking area, they were immediately struck by the resort's authenticity: Thatched roofs and rich earth tones abounded at the entrance. Near the entry way, guests were greeted by a hearty "Jambo"! ["hello" in Swahili] from cast members dressed in traditional African clothing. Indeed, many of the cast members working at the resort came from a variety of African nations and worked as part of a cultural exchange program. They were more than happy to interact with guests and talk about their customs and way of life back home.

Animal Kingdom Lodge was designed in the shape of a horseshoe. Known as a "kraal," African villagers use this type of design to keep their homes and livestock safe from predators.

At first blush, the lobby is an awe-inspiring sight. It was designed by the late architect Peter Dominick of Denver, who also designed the lobbies at Wilderness Lodge and Grand Californian resorts. He was selected for his talent, of course, but as Marty Skalr explained, also because of his close association with Joe Rohde:

> He and Joe had a great relationship. They even traveled to Africa several times.

Once inside the lobby, which is actually on the third floor of the six-story complex, syncopated drum beats reverberate, setting a festive tone. The lobby itself is massive, with large wooden beams supporting the roof structure. The light fixtures hanging from the roof are crafted out of authentic-looking shields and spears. The check-in area is covered by a large thatched roof. Natural dark wood floors, fences, benches, wooden tables, and chairs accentuate the earthy atmosphere. Sprinkled throughout the lobby are display cases, each holding rare and authentic African artifacts. In fact, more than 800 pieces of hand-made African artwork are on display throughout the resort, most notably in the lobbies and along the hallways. Near these displays, traditional African sayings and proverbs are etched on walls behind them. Perhaps the most interesting artifact on display is a 16-foot-tall and 8-foot-wide Agbo Ijele mask, created by the Igbo people of Nigeria in 1983. The mask is used only during important events and celebrations and is the only one of its kind in the world. Other artifacts include a feathered hat used by the Bafut people of Cameroon; an initiation hat used by the Pande people of Congo; and authentic headdresses and tools.

Rohde said:

> We owe it to future generations to preserve these magnificent treasures. I'm struck by the incredible attention to detail here.

As you make your way across the lobby, your eyes are drawn to large bay windows up ahead. High above, there's a wooden footbridge that crosses from one side of the fifth floor to the other. It's called the Maasai Bridge. Near the giant windows you'll find a staircase leading out to the resort's pride and joy— its own savannah. It's here where Animal Kingdom Lodge is set apart from just about any other resort in America. A short walk puts you out onto the savannah's large viewing deck, known as Arusha Rock. From the deck, guests young and old watch as giraffes stroll within 20 feet. Nearby, zebras munch on food, wildebeests shade themselves under trees, and ostriches stride along with nary a care in the world. There are more than 200 animals and birds from 30 species roaming freely over the massive preserve, many unique to the resort. Animal guides, most from Africa, are stationed on the viewing deck, happy to answer questions and share their expertise. Two other overlooks are also available to guests: the Sunset Overlook, located off the main lobby, and the Uzima Overlook, near the Uzima Pool area.

The success of Animal Kingdom Lodge spurred a major expansion, completed in 2009. The original resort was renamed Jambo House, while the newer section, Kidani Village, became part of the ever-expanding Disney Vacation Club portfolio.

(Jambo House has some DVC-dedicated rooms and, in fact, has a concierge level open to both DVC members and paying guests.) Kidani, which means "necklace" in Swahili, carried on similar traditions introduced at Jambo House, particularly with its own collection of African artwork. Indeed, there are numerous recessed shelves and alcoves located in the hallways of both resorts where pieces of art are on permanent display. In addition, the walls are sprinkled with African sayings and proverbs, from the humorous to the inspirational.

Much like Jambo House, which was designed to resemble a horseshoe, Kidani Village carried on the animal theme as it was built in the shape of a Cape buffalo's horns.

There are two savannahs located on Kidani's grounds: Sunset, which overlaps with Jambo House, and Pembe. Like Jambo House, Kidani Village also has its own observation deck (the Savannah Overlook) which protrudes into the savannah from the first floor.

While Kidani's lobby is much smaller than Jambo House's, its entryway is no less spectacular. And Kidani, too, has a large window at the rear of the lobby, offering stunning views of the savannah. Jambo House and Kidani Village are connected by a walkway, allowing guests who don't mind walking about 15 minutes access to both properties.

Joe Rohde had a hand in designing Jambo House and Kidani Village, although a little less so with the latter. When it came to Kidani Village, he said:

> I was like a professor emeritus. They asked me for my input. To me, Kidani Village is a continuation of what was started at Animal Kingdom and Jambo House.

There's rhyme and reason for the artwork featured in each resort. Jambo House is themed to man's relationship to animals. Kidani Village focuses more on the expressions of African people. The artwork on display at Jambo House and Kidani Village comprises the largest collection of African art outside of Africa.

Many of Animal Kingdom Lodge's rooms have savannah views, affording guests the opportunity to watch the animals from the comfort of their balconies. It's not unusual to see giraffes dropping to their knees late at night near a small pond.

It is a sign that they are relaxed in their environment. Guests, from either their room balconies or in designated viewing areas, watch a broad mix of animals and birds roaming freely, including Ankole cattle, zebras, roan antelope, Thompson's gazelles, giraffes, okapi, white-bearded wildebeests, ostriches, impalas, African spoonbills, and African greater flamingos.

One of the unique elements employed at both Jambo House and Kidani Village are hand-crafted African shields on the doors of every room on property. The shields draw inspiration from those used for centuries by the Maasai tribes of Kenya and Tanzania. Disney commissioned Maasai and Makonde artists to create them and they used implements such as machetes, knives, and sharpened screwdrivers to hand-carve the shields into four distinctive designs.

Construction of Jambo House and, in particular, Kidani Village, presented an unusual challenge to Disney's work crews: building a world-class resort without disturbing the animals. Imagineer Joe Legar said:

> We worked in close collaboration with our partners at Disney's Animal Programs to ensure that our construction activity didn't interfere with animal care. Animals don't like surprises, so when we needed to introduce new equipment to the project, we worked closely with the Animal Care team to set the equipment away from the savannahs. We gradually moved it closer so that the animals became familiar with it. Also, the Animal Care specialists didn't begin introducing new animals into the expanded savannah space until after we'd completed exterior construction.

Both Jambo House and Kidani Village feature expansive outdoor recreation areas, with massive pools serving as the centerpieces. Their pools have zero-entry areas and water slides. Kidani takes it a step further with a children's water play area, known as Uwanja Camp, which includes water jets, hoses, a waterfall and buckets keeping kids wet, cool, and entertained. Another unique feature at Kidani Village is the scores of covered parking spaces available to guests, a nice amenity on hot, sunny days or during Florida's famous mid-afternoon thunderstorms.

Both resorts have unique shopping areas (Zawadi Marketplace at Jambo and Johari Treasures at Kidani) which offer everything from clothing, jewelry, toys, and unique artwork. Many of the items for sale are themed specifically to Animal Kingdom Lodge. Often, native artisans will be on hand to demonstrate their skills in what best can be described as a vibrant straw-market atmosphere. Indeed, an entire cultural immersion program is offered at both resorts, which includes African face painting (in the Mara restaurant at Jambo House), medallion rubbing (in Jambo House's lobby), and pin trading (Zawadi Marketplace, Kidani Village). There's even a tour, starting at Johari Treasures in Kidani Village and led by a cultural representative, which gives guests insight into the design of Animal Kingdom Lodge.

Fine dining has been a cornerstone at AKL since its opening. Jambo House is home to two signature restaurants—Jiko and Boma—where the distinct culinary delights of continental Africa come to the fore. At Boma, guests are offered a buffet featuring a wide variety of African delicacies, such as bobotie (custard made with ground lamb), pap (African cornmeal), and fufu (mashed yam). There's also a carving station, where meat-lovers can satiate their appetites. For dessert, there are items such as the popular zebra domes and chocolate-coffee mousse confections. Jiko is located next door to Boma and features global cuisines on its menu, including leaf-steamed Chilean sea bass with asparagus puree, mushrooms, and apples; oven-baked garlic chicken tagine with grapefruit, olives and herbs; and a whole roasted papaya stuffed with spicy minced beef. Appetizers include cinnamon-spiced beef roll with vegetable-banana dip, and maize tamales with truffle oil, herbs, and spices.

For families, Jambo House offers a quick-service family restaurant known as the Mara, located just off its main pool. Burgers, salads, flatbreads, soups, a variety of African-inspired offerings, a grab-and-go section, and the ever-popular zebra domes are among the items available in the themed dining area. It's open for breakfast, lunch, and dinner. Victoria Falls Lounge, which overlooks Boma, is a richly detailed space where guests can enjoy a relaxing drink.

Kidani Village has one signature restaurant on property, Sanaa, as well as the Maji Pool Bar, where guests can grab a burger and a beer, among other quick-serve offerings, at poolside. Sanaa is the only restaurant on AKL property which offers guests a bird's eye view of the savannah as they dine. It's debatable whether you are watching the animals eat, or vice-versa. The design elements in all of Animal Kingdom Lodge's lavishly detailed restaurants are unique: light fixtures made to look like bird's nests, beads and gourds hanging from the ceiling, the branches of an Acacia tree dangling above, open fire pits where chefs prepare elements of each meal.

Sanaa presents the art of African cooking with Indian flavors. The dishes are inspired by flavors from Africa, the Middle East, Southeast Asia, and India. Spices play an important role in the foods featured at Sanaa, although "African spices are all about flavor, not heat," according to a member of the cooking staff.

In a real sense, Animal Kingdom Lodge is all about flavor, as well. It's a place that ignites the senses and strikes an emotional chord that few resorts come close to achieving. And the fact that it's a hop, skip, and a jump from the park from which it draws inspiration makes it that much more alluring.

CHAPTER THIRTEEN

Animal Kingdom at Night

Theme parks can develop reputations. People often form opinions of them after their first few visits and view them in a certain way. Those perceptions, whether true or false, tend to spread and hang over the park, for better or worse. For example, the Magic Kingdom in Walt Disney World is thought to be a great place for families with young children, even though thrill rides such as its famous mountains—Space, Splash, and Big Thunder—are among its most popular attractions. Epcot is perceived as more of an adult-oriented venue, with most shows and attractions geared to Baby Boomers. For the longest time, Animal Kingdom was viewed by many to be a half-day park. Guests would arrive bright and early, hop on Exhibition Everest, DINOSAUR, Kali River Rapids, and Kilimanjaro Safaris, then exit by lunchtime and head to another park. In those guests' minds, there wasn't enough to see and experience to justify staying past 1 or 2 o'clock in the afternoon.

And that, of course, was a shame.

Disney's higher-ups were aware of the phenomenon and, over the last few years, have made a concerted effort to change that perception. Beginning in 2015, Animal Kingdom began the arduous process of transitioning into a more enticing day-and-night experience. Several attractions were updated to reflect that change, while new attractions have been added to make Animal Kingdom *the* place to be after the sun sets.

Animal Kingdom has always reflected the evolving natural world. In that world, Joe Rohde said, "when day transitions into night, *everything* changes. Night is part of the cycle of life."

Kilimanjaro Safaris was one of the first featured attractions to receive an after-dark makeover, which was introduced during the spring of 2016. Indeed, the safari takes on a whole new dimension when viewed in the dark as the once out-and-about, always visible animals now seem to be lurking in the shadows, semi-hidden by bushes and trees. "At sunset, the animals seem to get more alert: it's hunting time!" explained Rohde. In an effort not to frighten the animals (and similar to its policy of never shooting off fireworks in or near the park), Animal Kingdom frowns on the use of additional lighting and flash photography during the night version of Kilimanjaro Safaris. That means spotting some animals, who naturally blend with their surroundings and are tough to spot even in daylight, can be difficult. Still, the sight of several giraffes dropping down to their knees as they prepare for a night's rest or other animals quietly grazing under the stars is magnificent.

One technological marvel was added to the safari: as the vehicles leave the thick forest area and enter the vast savannah, off in a distant stand of trees, there's a sunset...a spectacular lighting effect that is a sight to behold, punctuated by brilliant yellows and reds. Also along the safari route, several new animal enclosures, housing hyenas and wild dogs, have been added to the broad mix of creatures already on site. While some of the animals are a little tougher to see in the dark, many are more accessible at night and a bit friskier, including the lions, who seem to be more active than usual once the sun has gone down.

Indeed, keeping a mindful eye on the park's animals *and* offering guests new and innovative night-time experiences was a big challenge for Disney's creative team, but they met it head-on with some bright ideas that now play out nightly.

In the Asia section of the park, in the shadows of the popular Expedition Everest coaster ("imagine riding *that* in the dark!" is how one Disney executive put it), a new and exciting experience made its much-anticipated debut in early 2017. Rivers of Light truly embodies Animal Kingdom's new emphasis on the nocturnal and helps park guests celebrate night in an awe-inspiring way. According to Rivers of Light producer Michael Jung, the show's "light and sound pay homage to all living things."

Rivers of Light takes place on a large, oval-shaped portion of Discovery River, near the bridge that connects Expedition Everest and Finding Nemo: The Musical. A two-sided lakeside amphitheater was constructed, with each side seating about 2,500 guests on sturdy wooden or cement benches. As you take your seat, you notice four giant floating lotuses on the water. These lotuses are the focal point of the show and, as Jung stated, help "awaken the magic of nature."

The lotuses change color throughout the show, and even spread their petals and spray water. They are remote controlled and are joined by elaborately designed barges and floats which feature several wild creatures, including an elephant and a tiger. Behind them, as beautifully themed music plays, projections displayed on huge water screens tell a stirring story.

"Rivers of Light took more than three years to put together," explained Jung. He added that the show projects, many of which were taken from Disneynature footage, "are the essence of life...that every moment is a gift." Indeed, one of the stirring messages imparted during the show is the ancient belief that when as animal dies, its spirit rises into the heavens to become part of the aurora borealis.

The show takes its inspiration from World of Color in Disney California Adventure, in that it uses multi-colored lighting, music, and images projected on sky-high water screens to convey its powerful message. Ground-breaking technology, like cutting-edge LED lights and projections, is employed during the show. Rivers of Light was expected to debut in the spring of 2016, but problems getting those high-tech advancements to behave on a consistent basis delayed its opening for several months. Still, judging by the size of the crowds the show draws each night, it was worth the wait.

Another nocturnal attraction was added in 2016 that drew rave reviews from the outset. Called Tree of Life Awakenings, the colorful projection show can be seen from Discovery Island. It celebrates nature, as well as some highly recognizable Disney animated animal characters, with figures from *Bambi*, *Finding Nemo*, *The Jungle Book*, and *The Lion King*, among others, taking turns on the tree's massive trunk and limbs. If the music seems a little subdued, it's in deference to the animals populating the property. The show lasts about 10 minutes and runs from 9 p.m. until the park closes.

Also on Discovery Island, three distinct and entertaining shows are staged nightly across from Flame Tree Barbecue: Carnivale, with four shows running from 7:05 p.m. to 10:10 p.m.; Sunset Serenatas, six shows staged from 3:10 p.m. through 7:30 p.m.; and the Viva Gala Street Band, which performs three times in the evening, at 4:00, 4:50, and 5:40 p.m.

In the village of Harambe, additional food, beverage, and entertainment options have been added to accommodate the influx of night-time visitors. Harambe Wildlife Parti takes place nightly near the Mombasa Marketplace. As the sun sets, a bevy of singers, dancers, and acrobats set up shop, performing intermittently from 5 p.m. to 11 p.m. The last Festival of the Ling King show of the day starts at 8 p.m.

In Pandora, where even the walkways glow in the dark, the Swotu Waya Na'vi Drum Ceremony brings night-time entertainment to new heights. The exciting performers take the stage in the Valley of Mo'ara and under the shadow of the floating mountains nine times daily, from 10:30 a.m. to 9:30 p.m. As you might expect, the performances after dark are particularly magical.

In fact, Pandora is the ultimate in after-dark entertainment, with its bright, bioluminescent forest conveying the spirit of adventure, excitement, and color in the night-time world.

CHAPTER FOURTEEN

Pandora:
The World of Avatar

There's a line in the movie *Avatar*, spoken by all the natives of Pandora, that is deep and profound and embodies all that the fictional Na'vi culture embraces: "oel ngati kameie," or "I see you," which, loosely translated, means someone sees both your outer self and your inner being.

James Cameron, *Avatar*'s creator, first conjured the magical, mystical world of Pandora in a dream when he was a teenager. As an adult, after years of painstaking work, he translated that vision and presented it on the silver screen in 2009. What resulted was the highest-grossing movie of all time.

With the opening of Pandora: The World of Avatar in Disney's Animal Kingdom on May 27, 2017, guests could now see Cameron's vision, too, as well as feel, touch, taste, and immerse themselves in a magical, mystical, unique, and highly evolved world.

When the project was announced in 2011, Joe Rohde said:

> When I think about the Avatar story and Disney's Animal Kingdom, I see the value systems that underlie both.

Avatar producer Jon Landau said:

> The idea that we could create a theme park attraction that matched philosophically the movie's themes was not something Jim and I had thought about, but made perfect sense when it was presented to us.

Added Imagineer Lisa Girolami:

> We took cues from the film, but if there's an opportunity to talk about things that are bigger—ecology, conservation — this [Pandora] is it.

After construction on the new land began in 2014, Rohde said:

> We have the opportunity to tell that story in a way that will make the Avatar experience feel like a natural part of Disney's Animal Kingdom. Avatar is a uniquely suited property to live at Animal Kingdom.

During preliminary planning and development stages, Pandora was going to be just one attraction. But as the Imagineers sank their teeth into the project, they realized the collaboration between Disney and Cameron's Lightstorm Entertainment production company could conjure so much more. They ditched the single-ride concept and swung for the fences. The result? A home run of epic proportions, all contained within the largest expansion in Animal Kingdom's history.

As Jon Landau put it:

> [Pandora is] a remarkable technical and aesthetic achievement...that conveys a sense that it's alive, that it's a living place.

Added Disney Imagineer Matt Beiler:

> This is the first Disney land that tells a single story and we want you to be fully immersed in that story. We think that the story is seamless throughout Pandora.

What guests see first, even as they are approaching the park from the Osceola Parkway, are the incredible floating mountains, which now dominate the landscape to the left of the park's entrance. Like the snowy peaks of Expedition Everest and the Tree of Life, Pandora's floating mountains are a calling card and, even from a distance, one can detect the incredible detail that has been carved into these seemingly gravity-defying structures.

Pandora occupies the land that once was home to Camp Minnie-Mickey. It can be accessed from Discovery Island, as well as over a wooden causeway from Harambe Village in Africa, near where the uprooted Festival of the Lion King show is now located. Indeed, the placement of the boardwalk-like walkway suggests that Festival of the Lion King will always be linked to its original home, much in the way banshees are linked to the Na'vi on Pandora.

You need not have seen *Avatar* to appreciate the ecological message conveyed by Pandora...or its wondrous landscape, its bioluminescent magnificence at night, or its two signature attractions. But it certainly helps.

As you walk across the brand new, but wonderfully aged, rusted, and moss-covered bridge from Discovery Island to Pandora, you travel some 4.4 light years and are transported to a time when humans and the Na'vi (the indigenous people of Pandora) are at peace. Gone is the Resources Development Administration (RDA), an irresponsible mining company that was bent on extracting Pandora's valuable natural resource (unobtanium) without regard to conservation or the tall, blue-skinned creatures who occupy the land. Guests to Pandora now find Alpha Centauri Expeditions (ACE), an eco-tourism company that transports humans from Earth to the lush Valley of Mo'ara on Pandora.

Guests walking into Pandora will see, hear, and sense changes with each step. The plant life, for example, begins to take on an otherworldly quality. Hidden deep in the wooded area along the pathway, obscured by vines and foliage, are the remnants of a downed RDA helicopter, conveying the message that, in the end, nature will always win out. Closer inspection reveals that some of the trees and plants have been damaged, presumably by the some of the large Pandora creatures that roam through the foliage. As you walk closer to Pandora, you notice the ground contains subtle swatches of color; there also are leaf impressions and footprints in the concrete. Creatures can be heard in the distance, and it's up to you to surmise whether they're emitting loud shrieks to welcome you or to warn others of your presence. At night, the far-off creature sounds seem a bit closer, a bit more ominous. Also at night, the entire valley springs to life in a kaleidoscope of color; the various plants and life forms glow, and the ground turns into a bioluminescent wonderland, creating "a profoundly different environment," says Rohde, one that is "deeply interactive"— and almost spiritual.

A few short strides later, your face breaks out into the classic eyes-up, jaws-down reaction as you behold a site that's both stunning and breathtaking: floating mountains—the so-called

Hallelujah Mountains from the movie—covered with vines, odd-shaped flowers, pods, and branches, with water cascading from above, splashing into waterways at ground level.

During the park dedication, James Cameron said:

> We didn't build sets of all this stuff when we made the movie, it was all on computer. To be able to walk around...we're literally on Pandora!

As with the park itself, research played an integral role in bringing Pandora to life and making it as realistic-looking as possible, which is difficult, especially when you take into account that *Avatar* was based on one man's vision of a fictitious world and realism is, well, in the eyes of the beholder.

Imagineer Mark LaVine, the lead writer for Pandora, said:

> We want you to feel like you've gone to an alien world that is so realistic that it has to be a real place. We love to put you in real places at Animal Kingdom.

In their never-ending quest for realism, teams of Disney Imagineers visited far-off places like the Zhangjiajie National Forest in China, Plitvice Lakes National Forest in Croatia, and Tana Toraja Regency in South Sulawesi, Indonesia, for inspiration. Craftsmen from Bali and Java were enlisted to work on thatched roofs, totems, and artifacts that lend an air of authenticity. And, it was only fitting that Zsolt Hormay, the chief sculptor for the Tree of Life, lent his considerable talents to the creation of Pandora's floating mountains. In addition to these stunning works on his résumé, Hormay also helped create Monument Valley's colossal rockwork in the Cars Land section of Disney California Adventure.

The Valley of Mo'ara is a botanist's delight, with, as Cameron put it, "a mix of plants from Earth and Pandoran foliage." The thing is, you may need a degree in plant sciences to distinguish between the two, the realism of the faux foliage is so convincing. Interspersed with the plant life in the valley is a gently flowing stream and a winding walkway.

There are two interactive elements located in Pandora which blend seamlessly with the environment. The first is a natural drum circle, which consists of stone structures with hollow skins where guests can create their own thumping rhythms. Periodically, Disney cast members perform on the drums in what is known as the Swotu Waya ("Sacred Place of Song") Na'vi Drum Ceremony. The second, Flaska Reclinata, is a native Pandoran plant which looks like something right out of *Little Shop of Horrors*. It stands about 15 feet tall and is about 20 feet wide and when you "pet" it, the plant lights up and sprays a gentle mist of "spores" which, on a hot day, is quite refreshing. There's also a replica of an AMP [Amplified Mobility Platform] vehicle, a painful throwback to the days when the RDA tried to ruthlessly overrun Pandora.

There are two buildings, both designed to look as if they were once RDA facilities, that have been procured by Alpha Centauri Expeditions and now serve as a gift shop and a restaurant in Mo'ara. The Satu'li Canteen (a Quonset hut that once served as the RDA's mess hall) specializes in "local" cuisine, which means a wild variety of healthy, if somewhat exotic, Pandoran fare is on the menu. There's salmon and wood-grilled chicken, but also cheeseburgers encased in dough, vegetable curry bao bun, and spiced fried tofu. The colorful desserts include blue, yellow, and white cheesecake. The gift shop, known as Windtraders, has some of the most unique items for sale throughout Walt Disney World, including your own personalized banshee, which rests on your shoulder and can do things like scream and flap its wings. In addition to a host of Pandora-exclusive clothing and collectibles, you can also purchase 12-inch Na'vi figure that can be made to look like you, much in the way Jake Sully and the other scientists are transformed from human beings to Na'vi in *Avatar*.

In addition, there's a small refreshment stand called Pongu Pongu, where many of the colorful drinks glow in bright, bioluminescent splendor. Even the restrooms (one near Windtraders, the other near the entrance to the Na'vi River Journey) are heavily themed to Pandora.

By far, the main focus of everyone walking into Pandora is Avatar: Flight of Passage, one of the most lavishly detailed and exhilarating attractions ever created by Walt Disney Imagineering. According to Imagineer Diego Parras:

> This E-ticket attraction is the centerpiece of Pandora. It allows guests to soar on a banshee over a vast alien

world. The spectacular flying experience gives guests a birds-eye view of the beauty and grandeur of the world of Pandora on an aerial rite of passage.

On the attraction, you get to experience what it feels like to fly while seated on the back of a banshee. Under the cover of the floating mountains, guests enter the long queue (it's about one-third of a mile) and begin an imperceptible, winding trek upwards. The show building is an old RDA facility, and as such, is without upkeep and looks tattered and worn. In fact, during sections of the queue, there's exposed rebar, much of it covered in moss, and crumbling concrete walls. There also are overgrown vines permeating through the outside of the queue.

Once inside the main building, guests walk through a "ritual cavern," where drawings of Na'vi and banshees are etched onto the walls (and inspired by Native American cave paintings), suggesting how long the Na'vi have experienced these rituals of flight on the backs of the massive winged creatures, also known as ikran. There also are stingbats, native to Pandora, lurking in the cave. Guests then enter an area that resembles an underground bunker, with steel doors and concrete walls. Once through that section of the queue, guests walk past a bioluminescent section where foliage and rocks glow brightly. A sign near the rockwork identifies the Mountain Banshee Project.

From here, guests enter a laboratory, similar in design to the lab occupied by Dr. Grace Augustine in the movie. Several experiments are being conducted, including a display of the pesky Velocivirus, which is not native to Pandora, and whose origins are unknown.

Joe Rohde explained the creature's backstory:

> It survives space travel on transport vehicles, which are supposed to flare their thrusters before entering the atmosphere to burn it out. Of course, that takes fuel, and costs money, so not everybody does it. As with many introduced species, nobody has quite figured out how to eradicate it yet. The biologists of the Pandora Conservation Initiative are desperately trying to find a way to kill this thing, just one of the charming legacies of the exploitative reign of the RDA. Of course, there are also beautiful floating mountains, bioluminescent

flowers, flying creatures, and a wonderful indigenous culture, but this little phenomena appeals to my dark sense of humor.

There's also a piece of unobtanium (the object of the RDA's fanatical quest) on display.

Easily the most eye-catching element of this section of the queue is a 10-foot long blue Na'vi avatar encased in a giant tube filled with bubbling liquid. There also are workers' desks, where a variety of Pandora-related books, lunch boxes, and other items are within arm's reach. There's even a poster announcing an upcoming company softball game.

After exiting the lab, guests walk up another incline and enter an area where they are "scanned" to find an avatar that they are best matched with genetically. It's here where we meet Dr. Jackie Ogden, who has been the supervisor of these banshee flights for several years. Although her character is fictitious, she is based on a former Animal Kingdom executive.

Scott Terrell, currently the director of Animal and Scientific Operations at the park, explained:

> The scientist you see in the queue, Dr. Jackie Ogden, is actually an homage to the woman who was vice president of Animal Sciences at Animal Kingdom for many years. When we took Jackie to the attraction and she walked through the queue, she was really touched. When she heard her name, she actually broke down and cried.

After you've been linked to your avatar, you board your own "banshee." You'll take a seat in what is called a "link chair," which resembles a small motorcycle. There are handles in front and once you've put on your 3D glasses, three restraints (one at your back and two at your calves) gently lock you in place. The ride itself is similar to Soarin' Around the World, the popular motion simulator in Epcot and Disney California Adventure, with a dash of Star Tours from Hollywood Studios thrown in. On Soarin', though, guests are seated at ground level and the chairs are lifted some 60 feet into the air, until you're in front of a domed projection screen. On Avatar: Flight of Passage, all that gentle uphill walking you've done along the queue gets you to the necessary elevation without you even realizing it.

After several anxious moments and a short countdown, the metallic wall in front of you rises, white spots appear before your eyes, and you are transported to Pandora while seated on the back of your jittery banshee...and high up on a Pandoran cliff, at that. Your banshee pushes off the cliff and takes flight, soaring unsteadily through tree limbs and floating mountains. You fly side to side, swoop up, then straight down until you approach the shoreline of an ocean, where you come within a few feet of colliding with a giant whale-like creature as it leaps out of the water. You glide under a giant wave as a gentle mist sprays your face. After a few more harrowing near misses through another forest, your banshee comes to a stop. As it does, you can feel it breathing heavily underneath you. A musty, earthy smell permeates the area. Eywa, those tiny Pandoran creations revered as deity by the Na'vi, come floating by.

Amy Jupiter, one of the attraction's designers, said:

> You've come to a stop in a bioluminescent cave. You realize at this point that you actually know how to control the banshee. You know how to fly!

Then off you go again, gliding with other banshees through more harrowingly close encounters with Pandora's natural wonders before your flight ends.

Perhaps the most amazing aspect of the exhilarating experience—considering that you feel as if you've traveled for miles and miles, up, down, and all around—is your link chair never leaves its perch (although the floor itself does move out a few feet into the projection dome). Yes, it tilts from side to side and lurches forward and backward, but you remain stationary. Thanks to a barrage of sensory cues—including the mist in your face, the scent of dirt, the whooshing sounds of wings flapping and, of course, what you take in visually—each rider experiences a truly realistic flying experience. In the immortal words from the Disney classic *Peter Pan*: "You can fly! You can fly! You can fly!" On Avatar: Flight of Passage, you really can.

Also located underneath the floating mountains is Pandora's other main attraction, the Na'vi River Journey, which is the antithesis of Avatar: Flight of Passage: a gentle boat ride through a spectacular, wonderfully detailed bioluminescent forest. Along the way, projections of native wolves (they seem more curious of you than fearful or menacing) and Na'vi can be seen in the distance, peeking through the lush foliage. Other Pandoran entities, such as Eywa, float above your boat as you sail along. There are what appears to be the shadows of large bugs crawling on top of leaves dangling from above. The experience is meant to replicate the Na'vi way of life, the sense of being one with nature. It's very much an enlightening, quasi-spiritual journey.

The boats themselves, made to look as if they were crafted out of reeds, are smaller than the boats used in classic Disney water attractions like It's a Small World and Pirates of the Caribbean; at best, they seat three guests in two rows.

The ride culminates with the Shaman of Songs, who is perched on the shore of the river and goes through a series of intricate arm maneuvers and chants as you float past.

Imagineer Matt Beiler said:

> The shaman is the most technologically advanced Audio-Animatonics figure we've come up with to date. We wanted her to be as realistic and believable as possible. Her movements are so fluid; you can even see the emotion on her face.

Indeed, the emotions you experience throughout this enchanting new land are what make Pandora such a breathtakingly unforgettable experience.

Two days before Pandora opened to the public, dedication ceremonies were held in the shadows of the floating mountains. On hand were Disney chairman and CEO Bob Iger, *Avatar* creator/director/producer James Cameron, *Avatar* producer Jon Landau, Imagineering's Joe Rohde, and many members of the blockbuster movie's cast.

Rohde told reporters:

> [Pandora] is like visiting an entire world of adventure and experience really like nothing on Earth. First, it's completely beautiful. Second, guests have the opportunity to have a truly immersive experience...as if you are on another planet.
>
> Flying on the back of a banshee across the extraordinary beauty of this planet is just the most remarkable experience we can offer our guests.

In dedicating the new land, Iger said:

> At Disney, we have a "how did they do that?" standard. We love to build things that, when people look at them, they say, "How did they do that?" I cannot think of a better example of that than what we're standing in front of right now. We've been looking forward to this moment for quite a long time and we're thrilled we have a chance to share it with all of you. Walt Disney famously said that it's kind of fun to do the impossible and it's a sentiment that captures the soul of our company, reflecting the optimistic spirit in everything we do. Disney has been doing the impossible for almost a century now, thanks to the visionaries and innovators that have gigantic ideas, great courage, and the sheer will to deliver the impossible.
>
> Of course, at Disney, we call these people Imagineers. They turn bold ambitions into incredible experiences that only Disney can create. Special thanks to the creative and spiritual leader of this great land, Joe Rohde.

Turning to *Avatar* creator James Cameron, Iger said:

> Jim Cameron could easily be a Disney Imagineer. With big dreams and bold ideas and the immense drive necessary to see his visions come true, he does the impossible again and again and again. Merging wonderful storytelling with mind-blowing technology to create places that no one's seen before, and *Avatar* is definitely one of them. From the moment I first saw the film, I believed that Pandora actually existed. It just felt so real to me. And I wanted to visit there, just like millions of other people whose curiosity and wonder drove *Avatar* into the record books, as the highest-grossing movie of all time. *Avatar* introduced us to a stunning new world, breathtakingly beautiful and exotic. And today, years after its release, it's still captivating us as we eagerly await its next chapter. No pressure, Jim.
>
> Working with Jim and his team at Lightstorm, notably Jon Landau, was a dream come true for all of us as we pushed the limits of creativity and innovation to bring the digital world of Pandora to the real world of Disney's

Animal Kingdom. And now, everyone, including me, who has ever dreamed of visiting this extraordinary world can explore its astonishing landscape and ecosystem, see the Na'vi, soar on the back of a banshee, and become part of the Avatar adventure. Pandora is just as great in person as it is on the screen. I've been here several times and had the chance to enjoy all that Pandora has to offer.

Iger then introduced Cameron to the audience, who began his remarks in the Pandoran language:

Oel ngati kameie, Oel ngati kameie…which means "I see you, I see you," and I really mean that. This is a spectacular day for me and thank you so much to everyone at Disney who made today a reality. You know, I think back to when I was 19 years old and I had a dream…a dream of a bioluminescent forest with glowing trees and little spinning, glowing fan lizards and I woke up very excited and I painted it. I remembered those images years later when I started writing the script for *Avatar*. And then we made the movie. And here we are, years later, literally a dream has come true all around me. It's an amazing experience.

Joe Rohde and the incredible Imagineers have exceeded my wildest dreams in bringing Pandora to life. Thanks to this incredible collaboration, we can now walk through Pandora and learn all about the Na'vi and the Na'vi culture and the Na'vi's spiritual connection with their world. And that means Disney's Animal Kingdom, which is based on a deep respect for nature, is the perfect place to connect Pandora to our world. Disney's Animal Kingdom inspired us to understand and respect the natural world and our place in it.

Two days later, on May 27, Pandora officially opened. If the length of the lines and extensive wait times were any indication, the new land far exceeded everyone's expectations, which were set pretty high to begin with. In the weeks that followed, it was not unusual to see wait times that surpassed five hours for the Avatar: Flight of Passage attraction and over three hours for the Na'vi River Journey. The park extended its evening hours past midnight to accommodate eager guests.

Even the souvenir shop, Windtraders, always seemed jam-packed with guests (in classic Disney style, guests coming off Flight of Passage have no choice *but* to spill into the store). Many of the Windtraders' merchandise, particularly a miniature banshee figure that sits on one's shoulder and is controlled remotely, quickly sold out. In fact, the store—which sells only Avatar-themed merchandise—has been so popular that there have been long lines outside just to get in to shop for souvenirs.

Current Attractions in Pandora

Highlights: Avatar: Flight of Passage, Na'vi River Journey

Dining: Satu'li Canteen, Pongu Pongu

Shopping: Windtraders

CHAPTER FIFTEEN

Extracurricular Activities

On its surface, Animal Kingdom is as unique and enjoyable an experience as you'll find on this planet. There's nothing wrong with buying your ticket and spending the day exploring the animal habitats and attractions sprinkled throughout the 500-plus acres. But like an onion, there are many layers to Animal Kingdom, and taking part in any or all of several "extracurricular" adventures (most of which involve an additional fee) can make your visit that much more rewarding.

For instance, Wild Africa Trek allows guests to partake of the park's many features from a boots-on-the-ground perspective...even if sometimes those boots end up being 50 feet *above* the ground, with menacing-looking crocodiles and hippos staring up at you: walking across two 150-foot-long rope bridges is part of the Wild Africa Trek experience. That, and trudging through often thick underbrush; getting unusually close to a variety of animals on the savannah in a flatbed, covered safari truck, where standing and taking photos is not only allowed, but encouraged; enjoying an African-inspired lunch from a rustic observation outpost which overlooks the vast savannah—all under the watchful eyes of knowledgeable guides.

Midway through the trek, the safari vehicle pulls up to an authentic hilltop lodge overlooking the vast savannah. Here, participants peer out over the landscape from a wooden deck. They observe the animals grazing on natural grasses and plants. It's peaceful, quiet, educational, and quite emotional.

There's a comfortable restroom located to the back of the building. During the half-hour stop, guests are served a tasty lunch themed to several regions in Africa. It's a respite that truly embodies the spirit and mission of Disney's Animal Kingdom…and it takes place not all that far away from the main areas of the park, where guests scream with delight on modern, high-tech thrill attractions.

Guests staying at Animal Kingdom Lodge's concierge level can take part in a similar adventure, called Sunrise Safari. On select days, adventurers board a bus at the resort early in the morning prior to the park's opening, which takes them through a back entrance of the park. After viewing many backstage areas, the bus drops off guests in Harambe, where they walk a short distance and board the same type of vehicle used for Kilimanjaro Safaris.

Although the vehicle traverses a similar track, it tends to make longer stops whenever an animal meanders close by. Unlike the standard Kilimanjaro Safaris adventure, the Sunrise Safari has a driver and a guide. The guide offers more extensive details and interesting stories during the trip. It's not unusual for the guides to relay personal experiences they've had with some of the animals you view during the tour. During one such encounter, a guide recognized a giraffe walking on the savannah. "I was lucky enough to have been there when he was born," the guide said, adding that she knew it was him by his odd-shaped ossicones, the horns on top of his head.

At the end of the safari, guests disembark the vehicle and walk to Pizzafari, located on Discovery Island, where they enjoy a delicious buffet breakfast.

Up close and personal animal experiences aren't limited to the park. A similar safari adventure can be enjoyed by Animal Kingdom Lodge guests during the evening. It's called the Wanyama Safari and it sets off on its adventure at sunset. Guests board open-sided trucks at the lodge and travel through the vast savannah, where again, guides give detailed descriptions of the exotic animals who populate the area. After the safari, guests enjoy a hearty meal at Jiko.

For guests who want to get a sampling of what the on-property restaurants Jiko, Boma, and Sanaa have to offer, there are free culinary tours which commence at 4 p.m. each day. During each tour, foodies get to sample some of each restaurant's signature offerings, the goal being to whet their appetites for a full-course meal. Guests also get to interact with chefs and learn a little about how the exotic food in each restaurant is prepared. In addition, the guides talk about the design elements used in each restaurant and how small, seemingly innocuous touches correlate with certain African traditions and customs.

Another great feature at Animal Kingdom Lodge—and it's free—is the availability of night-vision goggles, which allow guests to peer out into the savannah during the still of the night and follow the animals as they walk about and graze. Children especially enjoy this opportunity to peek in on the animals under the cover of darkness. Also at Animal Kingdom Lodge is a nightly marshmallow roast, held on the deck leading out to the savannah at both Jambo House and Kidani Village. Kids get to toast their own marshmallows over an open fire pit (under careful cast member supervision, of course).

Children also love to take part in the Wilderness Explorers program. Young Wilderness Explorers (the group was first made popular in the Disney/Pixar movie *Up*) sign in at any one of several locations throughout the park. They are given a booklet and are asked to complete several animal-themed challenges. Participants earn badges as they work their way around the park. It's an interactive adventure that is done at your own pace. The guides give demonstrations and ask questions, and the explorers learn. Kids who take part in the program tend to absorb information like a sponge. "Mom, did you know that flamingos are pink because they eat shrimp?" Of course, learning is the focus of the program.

There's one experience in Animal Kingdom that usually draws shrieks and howls of delight. She's not an attraction, per se, and you won't see her on any guide map...in fact, there's a good chance you won't see her at all. She's called DiVine and she's kind of a wallflower, someone who is quiet, unassuming, and blends in with the scenery. Literally.

DiVine is what you might call a street performer. She can be found between Africa and Asia or in the Oasis. She blends in with the scenery because, well, she *looks* like the scenery. DiVine is a cast member perched atop green stilts, and her body is covered in leafy green foliage, large berries, and vines.

She has been known to stand completely still at the bend of a pathway. When a group of guests walks by, she'll slowly move her "branches" or walk in front of them. Those guests usually respond by letting out screams of delight. DiVine's performances usually last about 20 minutes; it's the type of experience that's truly unique to Animal Kingdom, mostly because it would be difficult for her to "branch out" at the other parks.

In keeping with Disney's commitment to teaching responsible conservation practices to young people, Disney's Animal Kingdom Programs Conservation Day Camp, held during summer months, offers youngsters a rare opportunity to get up close and personal with a variety of animals. They also learn the key tenets of recycling and how to help the environment. Campers are taken to backstage areas where animal-care experts interact with them and offer a fun and educational experience. In addition to learning about the animals, including their care and feeding, campers get to ride on many of the park's thrilling attractions.

Until construction commenced on Pandora: The World of Avatar in 2015, Animal Kingdom hosted its very own road race/scavenger hunt/obstacle course event, the Expedition Everest Challenge. The five-kilometer, runDisney-sanctioned event was staged in and around Animal Kingdom. It was labeled as an adventure race because competitors were required to cover the 3.1-mile course, overcome several obstacles along the way, and take part in a scavenger hunt before they could claim their finisher's medal. Now that Pandora is open, rumors have persisted that the race will be making a comeback.

Runners who take part in the annual Walt Disney World Marathon stride through some of Animal Kingdom's most remote backstage areas before having the experience of running through sections of the park proper. The race starts on the roadway outside Epcot. Participants run through Epcot before heading up to the Magic Kingdom. Once through the Magic Kingdom, competitors run past the Grand Floridian Resort. Here, the course takes them down Bear Island Road at about the 13-mile point, where things get downright backwoods, with a seemingly endless array of trees, grasses, streams, and thick brush lining the road. After a few miles of this bland landscape, Animal Kingdom's backstage buildings come into view. Runners enter the park near Harambe, then head toward Asia, past Theater in the Wild, and then through DinoLand U.S.A. before exiting the park through the parking lot. Many runners stop to take photos at the temple in Asia overlooking Discovery River, with Expedition Everest prominent in the background.

CHAPTER SIXTEEN

Wild About Animal Kingdom

Since it opened in 1989, Disney's Animal Kingdom has captured guests' imaginations in ways that even the most prescient Imagineers couldn't have imagined. Imagine that: a new species of theme park that touched on entertainment, conservation, environmental concerns, and of course, animal preservation...and touched people's hearts along the way.

For this final chapter, I decided to open it up to family, friends, colleagues, Disney cast members, and Disney fans in general, asking them to share their thoughts and favorite memories of a park that's truly one-of-a-kind and often tugs at guests' emotions. During his 54-year career with Disney, and even during his retirement years, Marty Sklar always appreciated hearing guests' feedback. He would have loved the gems below.

Thanks to all those who contributed their wonderful stories about Animal Kingdom...and a special word of thanks to my wife, Janet, for helping to compile many of these insightful observations.

Here, then, are what people are saying about Disney's Animal Kingdom Park as it approaches its 20th anniversary:

Nancy and Phil St. Pierre, Maine: Our grandchildren, Jack and Evie, became Wilderness Explorers by earning their badges as they roamed through Animal Kingdom. Part scavenger hunt, part outdoor classroom, it was an education filled with fun. Watching our usually bashful grandchildren ask the guides questions, or sometimes answering them, was a wonder to see. Memories of that special day in Animal Kingdom is something the kids still talk about.

Deb Wills, Florida: I still vividly remember the March day in 1998 that I spent in Animal Kingdom during cast previews... it was amazing! Around every corner was something new. The Tree of Life is magnificent. There really are no words to describe it. There are 350 carvings throughout the entire tree (and that includes the trunk, branches, and roots).

On that preview day, I watched artisans paint and became captivated during the Kilimanjaro Safaris, feeling like I was indeed in Africa; experienced Countdown to Extinction; saw Festival of the Lion King for perhaps my first of dozens of performances over the years. At dusk, as the cast members gently reminded us it was time to leave, I remember standing at the Tree of Life and softly crying. It was so moving and so beautiful. I still get chills thinking about it. There have been many changes over the years, but Animal Kingdom remains my favorite park at Walt Disney World. To this day, when I see the Tree of Life, I remember my thoughts and feelings from my very first visit.

Kelsey and Jason Beazer, Vancouver, British Columbia, Canada: On our first family trip to WDW in 2015, Animal Kingdom took us completely by surprise. We had not anticipated the fun and calming blend of adventure and wonder that we would experience there. Our hands-down favorite was the Festival of the Lion King show. Avery, our two-year-old daughter, was mesmerized by the talented acrobatic performers and the music. It felt like a Broadway show and was a wonderfully unique spin on a classic Disney film. Having grown up with *The Lion King*, we found such joy in seeing it anew through our daughter's eyes.

Paul Comstock, California: Joe [Rohde] was our inspiration. He's kind of the godfather of Animal Kingdom. Joe's big idea was to put people in with the animals. We all studied zoos and the company sent us around to look at a bunch of zoos and they were all basically the same: The animals are in a box and you're outside the box, looking into the box. Joe's thinking was to put the people inside of the box with the animals. And we'd make environments that looked like the people were inside the box looking at the animals.

Julian Robinson, Ontario, Canada: My best memory of Animal Kingdom did not occur at the park itself, but on Disney Cruise Line's *Disney Magic*. Imagineer Joe Rohde gave a presentation about the then-upcoming Expedition Everest expansion. The entire presentation was very interesting, as you would expect, but one point stood out for me. The Imagineers travelled to Tibet to study the local architecture and culture. Although they took a few photographs for reference, this activity is often confusing and alienating to the locals. When they sat down, they took out a sketchpad and started to draw what they saw—the local inhabitants see this as work and often come to see what they are doing and further interactions ensue. Those Imagineers not only know how to communicate with guests in Disney's Animal Kingdom, they can cover all types of communication even during the research and investigation phases.

"Exotic Bites," by Colleen Ann Myrhol:
Have a Yak and Yeti sandwich with me,
Followed by soup from the Flame Tree
Later we can munch at Pizzafari,
Or eat the delicious fruit of Harambe
Spend the day at the Kingdom with me,
I'll meet you at noon at the magnificent tree.

Mary and Bill Chatenka, New Jersey: In 2007, after dropping our youngest daughter off at college, we decided to take a much-deserved trip to Walt Disney World. No trip to Disney would be complete without a visit to Animal Kingdom. Naturally, we picked the hottest day of the year to go. We went from ride to attraction to ride. Finally, when we couldn't stand the heat any longer, we stumbled upon Finding Nemo: The Musical. It was a total surprise to us. The show was spectacular. It was cleverly done with colorful characters reminiscent of the Voyage of the Little Mermaid at Hollywood Studios. More importantly to us was the air conditioning, giving us a chance to cool down and rest.

Zofia Kostyrko, California: Since leaving Disney, I did some really fun stuff with Cirque du Soleil and Universal...all kinds of projects. I'm very eclectic in what I choose to do. I think that Animal Kingdom was such a high bar to follow. It did what a lot of parks didn't. It brought in the real-world issues in a way that grabbed people's hearts and motivated them to do something about it. If they care, they will make a difference.

Tracy Silvera, New Jersey: One of our daughter Abigail's favorite things to do at Animal Kingdom is the Wildlife Express Train ride to Rafiki's Planet Watch. It is a great break from crowds and a quiet hideaway for kids and adults to enjoy. The train takes you back to Conservation Station, where you can spend some time earning Wilderness Explorer badges and learn a thing or two about the different issues that are facing the animal world today.

When you are done, you can make your way outside to Animal Kingdom's own petting zoo, Affection Section. In this fenced-in area, you can find a variety of animals, such as goats and sheep, and even a pig or a llama. There are brushes available so you can show some TLC to these adorable animals, and sinks to use afterward to wash your hands. This hideaway is a great place to slow down your day and get a hands-on experience with some adorable animals.

Sandra and Jerry Duncan, Alabama: We took both our boys and their children for our first "grandchildren visit" to Walt Disney World and Animal Kingdom in December of 2007. All of us were enchanted by the Festival of the Lion King show. We were seated fairly close to the action, and our two 3-year-old grandsons were invited to join the parade at the end of the performance. Jack accepted; Spencer declined. Jack had a wonderful time marching around with the dancers and shaking his "native" rattle. When we were seated at Tusker House a short time later, we found that Jack still had his noise maker firmly grasped in his fist. I have no idea how he got out of there with the rattle (they are normally retrieved by the cast members), but I think he still has it almost 10 years later. Festival of the Lion King is a must for us, every time we visit Walt Disney World. But we've never scored another prop!

Jen and Alan Lai, California: The uniqueness of Animal Kingdom has always made it a special place for us to visit. We love that the live-animal aspect of the park ensures that no two visits are ever the same. Our favorite attraction is Kilimanjaro Safaris. You can ride it back-to-back and see a completely different set of animals each time. We have not yet had the opportunity to introduce either of our young daughters, Audrey and Sarah, to Animal Kingdom, but we know it will be a place that captures their attention and excites them tremendously. We can't wait for our next visit!

Linda Grierson, Washington: Living on the West Coast, Disneyland has always been our "home" park. Whenever our young children were scared by the animals on the Jungle Cruise or the immense boulder on the Indiana Jones ride, we would remind them that those things weren't real, just some of the wonders of Disney Imagineering.

However, on our first trip to Animal Kingdom park with our three-year-old son Jonah and our six-year-old daughter Hannah in tow, that changed. On our first ride, Kilimanjaro Safaris, there was a huge backup due to an animal on the road. "What, they're real?!", Jonah exclaimed. Everyone got a good chuckle as we explained that this Disney park was extra-special, because it had real animals to learn about and enjoy. We have been blessed with the opportunity to visit Disney parks on both coasts and in Paris, but Animal Kingdom holds a special place in the heart of our family.

I love having a place to teach my kids about amazing animals from far-away places, learn about conservation practices, and meet and talk to cast members from countries in Africa that we hope to visit some day, all while enjoying Disney magic in an immersive theme park.

Rick Sylvain, Florida: What resonates most for me about Disney's Animal Kingdom is the visual experience it is. It can be as simple as a prayer cloth in Asia or a termite mound on an African savannah, as grand as the Tree of Life or the floating mountains of Pandora. No detail is spared in transporting guests to exotic, faraway lands. The animal world, and our place in it, is celebrated here like nowhere else. For me, Animal Kingdom has always been a place of endless wonderment.

"Pandora," by Colleen Ann Myrhol:
Look all around you and don't miss a trick,
The waters are murky and the sand could be quick.

Keep your arms and hands always inside,
As you travel on your truly mystical ride.
Pandora is a strange land of adventure and magic,
Treat nature cruelly and the outcome could be tragic.
Respect all living things in our world and in all others,
And the ecosystems will repay you with amazing wonders.

Jason Lasecki, Illinois: I was an intern working in the Walt Disney World public-relations department when Disney's Animal Kingdom first opened. As a 20-year-old kid, to say it was a surreal experience would be an understatement. I was assigned the photo beat and worked with some of the world's best photographers to help them capture images of this amazing new park. I did all that I could to ensure the photos taken at the park were as spectacular as the park itself. I rode across Kilimanjaro Safaris at sunrise, capturing the giraffes grazing, elephants bathing, and lions roaring atop of the rock formation. A photographer wanted to take pictures of all the dinosaurs in the Countdown to Extinction ride, so I had the unique opportunity to actually stay overnight inside the attraction to assist.

Disney Magazine was looking to capture an image that would help show the immense size of the Tree of Life for its cover photo, so I donned a safari costume and climbed halfway up the tree to provide the needed scale. To this date, I think I'm the only person to ever be photographed climbing the Tree of Life. I had the magazine framed and love telling my kids the story of the day their dad climbed the Tree of Life.

Katie Caron, Maine: I love the subtle details within Animal Kingdom, the footprints and foliage, the creation of foreign lands feels so authentic.

Julie Sullivan, Massachusetts: The Wild Africa Trek at Animal Kingdom was an incredible experience. I was able to feed a hippopotamus, with the help of an animal specialist. I was so close to the hippos I could count their whiskers! The Wild Africa Trek is as close to being on an actual safari as you can get without traveling to Africa. It's an experience of a lifetime.

Tara Stewart, South Carolina: My four-year-old son Hayden is obsessed with bugs and anything related to insects. It's Tough to Be a Bug was a huge hit, from the stink bug "stinking" us to the bees and ants and how they help the environment. He loves learning and this show (and the movie *A Bug's Life*) teaches while being interactive and fun for kids of all ages. I could have done without the thought of roaches and maggots touching my bum on the way out, though!

The Kilimanjaro Safaris also was mesmerizing for my son. He couldn't believe that he was "this close" to all the animals he normally only sees in books. The opportunity to ride and see animals in what feels like an open setting was exciting and educational for him. It was one of the highlights of our trip.

My son loved the Boneyard dinosaur dig site. The staff sat with him and helped him get his shovel and pail and talked to him about dinosaurs and bones and he says all the time he wants to be an archaeologist so he can dig for bones. He was so content and it was the longest time we stayed in one place as it kept his attention; the staff took time and great care to engage him, and it was a cool break from the sun. The interaction gave him a sense of accomplishment in dusting off his part of the dinosaur and he felt like he had truly "discovered" something.

The stage shows Festival of the Lion King and Finding Nemo: The Musical are perfect for young children. The music and performers are so engaging and they had all the highlights from the movies that my son loves. And as an adult, these were my two favorite shows from the entire park because it's the music you sing for the rest of the day. We also had some of the best food in Walt Disney World at Animal Kingdom. There were more healthy options and a variety of food more like what we eat at home and we were happy to take a break and eat something other than pizza or hamburgers.

Michelle Craffey, New York: When my husband and I took our two daughters, Caitlin and Molly, to Disney World for the first time in November of 2011, we vividly remember their experience at Animal Kingdom. The park was perfect for their ages, and we were delighted with all the amenities it had to offer our family. One of our favorite recollections was when the girls had their faces artfully painted. They didn't want to wash it off and tried to keep it on for the rest of our stay. Fortunately, we had many pics to share and show them, so they would have those wonderful, magical memories for life.

Sue Dindia, Illinois: In 2010, when our grandson Kenai was 6 years old, my oldest daughter went to Somaliland with him to teach for a year at a boarding school in East Africa. While there, she taught at the high school and local university, and our grandson was befriended and tutored by the Somali students. He learned many native life skills; among them was how to negotiate for and skin a goat. They traveled extensively throughout Africa during the year. My husband Gary and I met them in South Africa and traveled to Botswana for a safari at an elephant preserve. We stayed at a resort in Zambia, within walking distance to Victoria Falls, and they had zebras roaming throughout the grounds. They also went on a safari in Tanzania on their way back to the school.

In June of 2014, Kenai (who was 10 at the time) and his best friend Trey Phillips flew from their home state of California to Chicago and the four of us went to Walt Disney World. Harambe Nights was a hard-ticketed event at Animal Kingdom featuring special entertainment, buffet-like food stations throughout the Africa section of the park, and lots of interaction with the international cast members. While meandering through the event area, Kenai noticed one of the cast members playing with a game he played in Somaliland called Layli Goobalay. The cast member challenged him to a game and our grandson quickly beat him. The cast member asked for a rematch, not thinking that such a young kid could actually beat him in this game of logic and strategy. Our grandson beat him again. The cast member asked him how he learned to play the game so well. Kenai and the cast member had a lovely conversation about East Africa and his year-long stay in the region. It was quite heartwarming.

Kenai also enjoyed the food offerings, which included items he had eaten over there—sambusas, rice with various herbs, and stew. Kenai's friend has a peanut allergy and I was most impressed that at each station, when asked, a chef would appear and explain what he could and could not eat. Typical Disney magic! Having been on several safaris in Africa, Kenai was nevertheless very impressed with Kilimanjaro Safari. He could easily identify many animals even before our guide pointed them out. He was amazed he could get closer to the animals at Animal Kingdom than he could while in Africa and gave the ride two thumbs up for its resemblance to the "real" safaris.

During Kenai's first visit to WDW when he was four, we stayed at Animal Kingdom Lodge. He was immediately entranced with our savannah-view room and spent hours on the balcony looking at and identifying the animals. Our daughter commented that we could have saved a lot of money by not buying tickets for the parks and just letting him spend all day hanging out on the balcony. He was quite sad on that trip that he was not tall enough for rides that had height restrictions... except for one. When he was measured and passed the "test" for Kali River Rapids, his face lit up, he pumped his arm in the air, and he grinned as if he had just hit a walk-off home run to win the World Series at Wrigley Field. Kali quickly became his favorite ride at all of WDW.

Jack Caron, 11, Maine: My favorite part of Animal Kingdom is the Tree of Life and looking for all the hidden animals in the trunk. I can look at it all day and find new creatures.

Cavrel Silvera, New Jersey: As a long-time *Avatar* fan, I was looking forward to the opening of Pandora. When I got the opportunity to join my father-in-law for a pre-opening press event, I knew I could not pass it up. I felt great anticipation leading up to the trip. I have seen the movie *Avatar* approximately 30 times (insane, I know), so I had a great visual of Pandora in my mind, and let me tell you, Disney's interpretation did not disappoint.

When I walked into Pandora for the first time, I noticed the ambient sounds. They were coming from every corner, and it helped transport me to Pandora. As I walked down the river path into the main entrance, I began to notice the vegetation, which were reminiscent of the movie. They were a mixture of indigenous plants, and what I can only assume were props, but it all looked very real nonetheless.

I finally made my way to the spectacular Hallelujah Mountains and then to the pièce de résistance of the entire experience, the Flight of Passage attraction. As I walked onto the elaborate queue, I was in awe of what the Imagineers were able to create. From the subtle to the not so subtle, they were able to capture the feel of Pandora. The Flight of Passage, simply put, is the most exhilarating experience I have ever had on any attraction. The sights, the sounds, the smells, were palpable...just *amazing!*

Anna and Gaspare Sabella, New York: We will never forget one of our Disney trips in August of 2009. We were there early for rope drop and were waiting patiently to be let in. Our family and my brother and his family were chosen as "family of the day." We were escorted to Kilimanjaro Safaris to be the first and only families on the attraction. Each of our families also was given a certificate. It was a sweet, magical moment for us.

We love Festival of the Lion King...truly a Broadway-quality show. For us, Animal Kingdom has many great food options. We also are looking forward to experiencing Pandora and the Avatar: Flight of Passage attraction.

Norma and David Englehart, Arizona: We love spending time at Animal Kingdom and have made some great memories there. The theming is all-encompassing, so there are no breaks in the adventure, whether we are on an exciting ride, enjoying some delicious food, or watching our favorite show, Festival of the Lion King.

Finn Dalton, 5, Texas: Animal Kingdom is my favorite place to be an archaeologist. Riding dinosaurs and then digging for dinosaur bones is the best.

Kara Cohen, 9, Florida: Disney's Conservation Day Camp is a great experience. You get to go backstage at Animal Kingdom and see roads and areas that most people never get to see. We learn all about animals and the different species. Every grade group does something different. I have gotten to meet a pony, touch a snake, meet a turtle, and I even went into a giraffe barn where no one ever gets to go.

As we learn about animals, we make them special treats. This year we made treats for a giraffe. Last year we made treats for a meerkat.

Kyle Dalton, 11, Texas: Animal Kingdom Lodge is the best hotel I've ever visited. You can learn about the animals, conservation efforts, and life in Africa while earning beads for a cool necklace. They also have s'mores every single night.

Evelyn Caron, 8, Maine: I had so much fun earning my Wilderness Badge and want to do it again. I saw all areas of the park that I wouldn't normally see when just riding the rides, and I learned a lot. Be sure to ask for the loud ceremony, not the quiet one, when you earn your badge. It's so fun!

"Kilimanjaro Safaris," by Colleen Ann Myrhol:
I climbed into my jeep and looked far ahead,
On a safari adventure to locate Big Red.
As I crossed the savannah I could see
All of the animals you could imagine to be.
There were giraffes, monkeys and crocodiles,
Hyenas, and hippopotamuses with great big smiles.
Antelopes and gazelles went speeding by,
And cheetahs were as fast as an airplane could fly.
We saw a majestic lion on the very top of a hill,
Glaring at men holding elephants against their will.
It's the Big and Little Red elephants we all shouted with glee,
Safaris are different now but that trip was as good as could be.

Rick Barongi, Texas: I think what I learned from Animal Kingdom was more about who to pick on your team, what type of people...to find keepers who like people as much as they like animals. If you're going to make an impact, you have to have the keepers tell their stories. Connecting the exhibits and the story was something Disney really upped the ante with. Disney also showed me that a for-profit company can also be a force for conservation, just as much as a non-profit. My commitment to conservation became even more after working for Disney.

David Cohen, Florida: Pandora is amazing. The detail is everywhere. You feel you have been transported to another world. The level of rock work, plants, moss, building decay, and everything else blows your mind. The standby line alone for Flight of Passage should be its own attraction. It's crazy that the FastPass users will miss it all!

The Na'vi River Journey was beautiful, but I felt it lacked a full story. It should have been a little longer. Overall, the parts there and the level of detail is just awesome. The frogs jumping on the leaf that make the leaf move is such a great add on. The level of depth in the projections of animals and Na'vi is great.

Avatar: Flight of Passage is breathtaking...just amazing how they enhanced the basic Soarin' concept. When you look behind you on your ride, you see how the ride is moving. Each link chair pitches left and right (maybe more), but the whole eight-chair room detaches from the walls and moves as well. Just astonishing how they could do all that.

The great thing about the whole land is you don't need any prior knowledge of the movie. They clearly thought of all that. If you know it, it adds to your experience. If not, they tell you what you need to know. Overall, just amazing.

Neil Johnson, Maryland: The moment we walked into Animal Kingdom Lodge, we felt warmth and welcome. It was definitely a feeling of being home.

Betsy Fischer, Louisiana: I was lucky enough to visit Animal Kingdom when it first opened. I think I still have the opening-day brochure. This park is unlike any other. For one thing, there are no plastic straws allowed here.

One of my favorite things to see at Animal Kingdom was Tarzan Rocks. The show was amazing with the skaters and acrobats. I was impressed at how the skaters could jump over the other skaters and not fall on them. My other favorite show is Festival of the Lion King. The question going into the show was would I get to be a lion, giraffe, warthog, or elephant? I never knew that giraffes made a noise that sounds like a sheep. This show is high energy—from the monkeys to the fire twirler. My daughter adored the monkeys and was excited that the zebra invited her to participate and be part of the show.

Kilimanjaro Safaris was always an adventure—would we stop the poachers in time? It was secretly educational in that everyone left the ride learning how to say "hello" in Swahili ("jambo") as well as learning about the animals. To me, the scariest part of the ride is driving over the crocodile area. To this day, I still hold my breath whenever we drive over the rickety bridge. The ride also guarantees that every adventure will be different because you don't know what animals will be close to your vehicle. Luckily, we only saw the lions from far away.

As my daughter has gotten older, I have been able to take her on DINOSAUR and Kali River Rapids. She is still amazed when she sees DiVine (although sometimes we have to really search for her as she is well hidden).

Kelly Castellano, New Jersey: I was sitting in the Festival of the Lion Show with my one-year-old son, Vincent. As we were enjoying the show, all of a sudden one of the Tumble Monkeys jumped right in front of us onto the seats. It startled us for a second, but after the initial shock, Vincent put a big smile on his face and even gave the Tumble Monkey a high five. It was a wonderful moment.

Hannah Johnson, 15, Maryland: I remember when we were small and we stayed at Kidani Village. Our room was close to the community center and our parents let us do art activities and sometimes we ran to the store to refill our resort mugs. It felt like freedom!

Dana-Mari and Joe Ciaranca, New Jersey: One of our favorite memories happened in the area formerly known as Camp Minnie-Mickey during the holiday season. Our boys were anxious to meet Mickey and his pals in their holiday attire. While we waited in line, we began talking to a gentleman with a guitar, who we later found out was Guitar Dan. He chatted with the boys and after finding out some details, Guitar Dan wrote a song about the boys called "The Christian and Nicholas Song." It was heard all throughout Camp Minnie-Mickey and we couldn't have been more excited for such a perfectly pixie-dusted moment.

Amelia Schmidt, 5, Delaware: I love seeing all the animals. They get so close to you. We saw the baby giraffe and the baby elephant when we were on the safari. They were so cute!

Kristen Johnson, Maryland: During one of our stays, we noticed a large eland who liked to sleep against a log not too far from our window. We named him Fred and each night before bed, the kids would run out on the balcony and call out, "Good night, Fred!" It was one of my favorite memories.

Kevin Rafferty, California: Pandora is kind of like Cars Land (in Disney California Adventure). If you haven't actually seen it, it's hard to explain what it's like. Unless you stand there and look around, you don't get a sense of how spectacular it is.

John Barber, Texas: When my wife Robin walked into Animal Kingdom Lodge's Kidani Village, she cried...overwhelmed by the beauty of the resort and savannah.

Leslie Kittlesen, New York: Animal Kingdom is my favorite theme park at Walt Disney World, due to the way I first saw it. My sister Susan and I were staying at Old Key West in 1998 when the front desk announced that resort guests could get a $25 ticket to go to the Animal Kingdom, which had not yet opened. I was thrilled and told my sister we had to go. The day before, my sister had a huge splinter removed from her foot, so she had to use a wheelchair for 24 hours, which was a blessing in disguise because it slowed us down.

The other blessing in disguise was that so few rides were open. We were completely charmed from the moment we got to the gate. We found the foliage so beautiful and the animals so fascinating that it took us almost two hours to get through the Oasis. Because it was a soft opening, there were very few people around, so it was incredibly peaceful as we moved through the paths. (I am often sad when I see people rushing through the Oasis to get to the "good" parts; they're missing so much!) Then we came over the hill and saw the Tree of Life for the first time. We literally stopped, stunned at how beautiful it was. We spent the next hour going around the tree and admiring all of the incredible carvings.

We headed to the back of the park and were transported to the savannahs of Africa on Kilimanjaro Safaris. Hunting down poachers and the element of surprise (it was our first time) made for a thrilling ride. The other thing that stood out was walking through the ruins of the maharajah's hunting lodge to see those magnificent tigers pacing around just feet from us. We felt transported to another place and time. All of this happened with a backdrop of really lovely music floating through the trees (I bought the Animal Kingdom "soundtrack" and still use it as a go-to when I want to relax). I had no idea that a theme park experience could feel so peaceful and grounding. It was a chance to step away from the hectic 20th century and move at a slower pace and look around. Even though the Animal Kingdom is more crowded and moves at a faster pace now, I am always able to slow down there and savor the peace.

Kristin, Lou, Matt, and Abby Bonasera, Massachusetts: The kids' favorite memories of Animal Kingdom include always going to the safari first to say "hi" to "Cannoli," which is what they named one of the Ankole cattle. They loved the Jingle Jungle Parade at Christmas and Abby still talks about the hot chocolate smell coming from Minnie's float. Our favorite pictures are of the kids dressed in their holiday outfits in Camp Minnie-Mickey. For my husband Lou and I, what is special about Animal Kingdom is teaching the kids about conservation, the environment, and especially how they care for animals. We've explained to so many ignorant people that Animal Kingdom isn't a zoo, and why. And of course, it's fun! I remember an early morning Magic Hour when the kids rode Expedition Everest four times in a row without getting off. Abby still squeals during It's Tough to Be a Bug when the ants crawl under your butts at the end.

Ryan Schmidt, 7, Delaware: I've seen *Avatar* a lot and I really love it. The first time I walked into Pandora, it felt like we were actually in the movie. The Na'vi River boat ride and Flight of Passage are awesome. I can't wait for LEGO to come out with Avatar sets. The first time we went to Animal Kingdom, I loved digging for dinosaur bones because I want to become a paleontologist when I grow up. I can't wait to bring my little brother Aaron to the dig site the next time we go.

"The Lodge," by Colleen Ann Myrhol:
You're the last person sleeping and everyone wonders why,
The doors are opened wide, so you'll hear birds flying by.
Your wife is having coffee on your beautiful veranda,
The kids are watching animals roam across the savannah.
Boma has just opened for a flavors of Africa buffet,
When breakfast is over, you can start out on your day.
After a leisurely stroll through the Animal Kingdom park,
Your family can learn and feast at Sanaa just after dark.
When the kids are safely tucked into their bed,
Sip wine at Jiko to plan your next adventure ahead.

Jess Dalton, Texas: There's a beauty within Animal Kingdom (park and lodge) that surpasses everything else inside Walt Disney World. From the stage shows to the restaurants, from the architecture to the massive art collection, there's nowhere else on property that so thoroughly transports me to another place. There's a serenity at AKL that I need after the stimulation of the parks. The lighting is softer, the colors warmer, the stories of the cast members are captivating, even the animals are relaxed and slowly grazing around. For us, it is much-needed down time as you are really immersed in the culture of Africa.

Amy and Shawn Goodall, Florida: I was blown away the first time I walked through the gates at Animal Kingdom. I had never experienced anything like it. The colors, the smells, the flowers...everywhere I looked, in every direction...amazing beauty! It overwhelmed every sense of my being. I kept asking myself how did they do this? And I had not even been on a ride yet. Our children (Rivkah, Josiah, Havilah, and Talyah) had bets going for many trips whether or not the crocodiles on the Kilimanjaro Safaris ride were real. Finally, one time when we were on the ride, a croc moved and we all screamed with excitement. Mystery solved.

We decided as a family to go to Animal Kingdom on opening day for Pandora. It will go down as one of our most favorite Disney memories. We waited in line to ride Avatar: Flight of Passage. We did not mind the wait because there was so much to look at and take in...the colors, the plants, the flowers... every tiny detail. We were like kids in a candy store. We all agreed Flight of Passage is the most amazing ride we have ever been on. We knew we had just experienced something special when we got off the ride.

Andrew Dalton, Texas: I feel completely taken away on my stays at Animal Kingdom Lodge and totally relaxed. For someone who will never have the chance to take the family to Africa, staying there is the next best thing. The cast and crew bring the resort to life and I feel totally immersed. It's by far my favorite.

Ryan Basedow, 10, New Jersey: My first roller-coaster ride was Expedition Everest. All trip I kept telling my dad I would go on it, then I chickened out. I finally rode it and as soon as we were done, we rode it again...in the front seat!

Greg Ryback, Tennessee: Animal Kingdom is the most unusual of all the Walt Disney World experiences in that most people don't know the back story. It's very easy to miss the details if you're not paying attention. After taking the Wild by Design VIP tour back in 2007, a whole new world was open because I then understood the theming throughout Animal Kingdom and it quickly became my favorite of the Disney parks. From Chester & Hester's Dino-Rama, to the "dorms" around the Dino Institute, to the themed rooms in Pizzafari, Animal Kingdom is literally filled with hidden gems.

Matt Basedow, 8, New Jersey: I don't like scary roller-coasters, so I won't ride Expedition Everest, unlike my brother Ryan. I love to play in the dinosaur boneyard and dig area; that's my favorite part.

Kelly and Mark Kichiy, Ontario, Canada: The memories of having been on safari in South Africa come back to us whenever we go on Kilimanjaro Safaris. It is something we do more than once during our annual expeditions to Walt Disney World. The ability of the Imagineers to capture the realism of our safari has always amazed us, and transports us back to the dark continent each and every time.

Talyah Goodall, 10, Florida: I love seeing all the real animals. Someday my folks will take me to Africa for a real safari ride, but this is definitely the next best thing.

Jeff Eckstein, New York: One of my favorite attractions in Animal Kingdom has always been Kilimanjaro Safaris. It is incredible that Disney has their own wildlife reserve, contributing to a solution of safe havens for so many animals. On the guided tour, you truly feel like you are in the middle of the savannah. It is just another piece of the Disney magic that amazingly transports us to another place.

Amelia Metz, 11, Pennsylvania: Animal Kingdom is an amazing Walt Disney World experience. It has very cool attractions/shows that involve things from your favorite movies such as *The Lion King* to a safari that takes you deep into the African savannah where lions roam. I can remember many things from Animal Kingdom. Recently, we went on the Flight of the Banshee ride from the film *Avatar*. It truly felt like virtual reality. You could feel the banshee breathing between your legs and when you dipped down low, you felt like you were truly falling. It was a fantastic thing to experience. Animal Kingdom may be very different from the rest of the parks, but it really stands out in a unique way.

Mandy Dyck, St. Catharine's, Ontario, Canada: My boys would tell you that the Boneyard is one of their favorite things to do while at Animal Kingdom. They would spend the whole day there if we didn't force them away to do other stuff.

In 2011, we had a larger family trip that included a grandma, a grandpa, an aunt, an uncle, and a cousin/niece. We happened to go to the park after a day that started off rainy, but this totally worked to our advantage as the park ended up being pretty empty. Our niece was four at the time and couldn't get enough of Kali River Rapids. The cast members were great and let my niece, her dad, and her grandpa ride over and over again without having to get back in line. That is a story that is told whenever we discuss that Disney trip.

One trip we went to see It's Tough to Be a Bug and ended up being robbed by a squirrel. We had some raisins that were still in the box, sitting in a Velcro-sealed section of our stroller console. The squirrel opened the section where the raisins were and took off with the box. Guess he was fed up with eating popcorn off the ground.

My favorite thing to do when visiting Animal Kingdom is to go on Kilimanjaro Safaris. I miss the anti-poaching storyline and I find the new version sort of boring; maybe it has more do with my guides. I'm really on the ride to see the animals and each safari is different, thanks to the animals, so I'm good. I've been fortunate enough to hear a lioness roar (multiple times during the same ride, which then got a little creepy since she is the hunter), to see a white rhino up closer than I ever expected, to be close enough to giraffes that I contemplated jumping out to give one a hug (I *love* giraffes!), to see a baby elephant, and to just see all the great animals in general. I'm also a big fan of the savannah-view rooms at Animal Kingdom Lodge. I could sit all day and just watch the animals from the balcony.

Sharon and Karl, Indiana: One of our first memories of Animal Kingdom came when we were in Africa on a path heading to Asia. A big crowd had gathered around and they were all looking at something, and you could tell the crowd was excited, but we couldn't tell what they were looking at. When we went back a couple of years later, and having read about it, we finally figured out what everyone was excited about: DiVine. She's very cool and a special Disney touch.

Jeremy Metz, 11, Pennsylvania: One of my favorite memories of Animal Kingdom was when I went on the Primeval Whirl for the first time. Everything about it was fantastic—the spinning, the sharp turns, and the sudden hills. I would happily suggest it to anyone at the Animal Kingdom.

Joe Rohde, California: It is my hope, and I believe all of ours, that we have created a place that will awaken our hearts to the beauty and wonder of the creatures that surround us, and renew our dedication to conserving those places on Earth where they may survive until a wiser time when we have learned the lessons of the Earth and can share in harmony with our partners on this small planet, the animals.

Acknowledgments

When I first came up with the idea of writing a book tracing the history of one of my favorite Disney theme parks, Disney's Animal Kingdom, my game plan was to tie in the development of the park with what was featured on opening day and then detail the changes the park has seen in the last two decades. That would be topped off, of course, with the opening of the spectacular Pandora: The World of Avatar in 2017. Once I formulated this plan, I went to my go-to Disney guy for his advice, encouragement, and wealth of knowledge.

Former Imagineering creative leader Marty Sklar has always been extremely giving of his time and expertise with me. When I approached him about this book, he was all in... so much so, that my enthusiasm seemed to become his enthusiasm. Just one day after I contacted him, he sent me a long email with an extensive list of people who were involved in the planning, concept, and design phases of Animal Kingdom. Not only that, but he gave me phone numbers and email addresses for all those wonderful folks. Without his help, this book just wouldn't have the depth and accuracy it deserves.

In November of 2016, I had lunch with Marty at the Wave in the Contemporary Resort at Walt Disney World. Joining us was Ryan March, editor of *The Disney Files* magazine, which goes out to Disney Vacation Club members. As we walked toward our table, we crossed paths with a rather high-profile group of people, including Joe Rohde (who had a mobile device pressed against his earring-less right ear the entire time and could only manage a wink and a nod) and Jon Landau, the producer of *Avatar* and *Titanic* and one of the behind-the-scenes forces involved in the creation of Pandora. Marty and Jon exchanged greetings and then Marty introduced me to Jon. "This is my friend, Chuck Schmidt. He's a newspaper editor and a fellow author." The two then proceeded to talk about the progress of the Pandora expansion for a few minutes. While meeting Jon Landau was exciting, and having lunch with Marty and Ryan was a true joy, being introduced as Marty's friend made my day; it's a warm feeling that has stayed with me.

On July 27, 2017, I was just a few weeks away from completing work on the book when I learned of Marty's death in Los Angeles at 83. A few weeks before his passing, I conducted a 45-minute telephone interview with him. He offered insight into his involvement with the Animal Kingdom as the leader of Walt Disney Imagineering. As usual, his memory was sharp as a tack, and his stories were on-point and thoroughly interesting. At the end of the interview, I thanked Marty for his time, and bid him well. It was the last time I'd speak to him.

My plan was to send him a copy of the finished version of this book, at which point I knew he'd give it a studious read. And I knew he'd pass along any of what he called "nits"—corrections and suggestions on what might have been problematic in his eyes and which would ultimately make the book better. Once the book had gone through his learned filter, I figured I'd be good to go. And I was looking forward to presenting him with a copy of this book for his collection.

That being said, this book is dedicated to *my* friend, Marty Sklar.

I would be remiss not to mention the Imagineers and Disney cast members, both present and former, who were so generous with their time and their great recollections, either in person at numerous press events over the years, on the telephone, or via email. Much thanks to Kevin Rafferty, Zofia Kostyrko, Paul Comstock, Diego Parras, Dave Bossert, Dr. Scott Terrell, Emily O'Brien, Michael Colglazier, Rick Barongi, Michael Jung, Matt Beiler, Zsolt Hormay, and of course, Joe Rohde.

My wife Janet and I have been advocates for animals for most of our 45-year marriage. In addition to our own pet crew—two dogs and five cats at last count, all rescues—we have fed the family of rabbits and the birds in our backyard, rescued wayward frogs from our pool, stopped the car in the middle of a busy road to help a turtle get across without harm, and donated to worthy animal rescues. As usual, a portion of the proceeds from this book will help support our favorite animal rescues.

About the Author

Chuck Schmidt was bitten by the Disney bug at an early age. He remembers watching *The Mickey Mouse Club* after school in the mid-1950s. During his 48-year career in the newspaper business, he channeled that love of Disney as the Sunday News and Travel editor for the *Staten Island Advance*, writing features and covering a variety of events involving the expansive world created by Walt Disney.

Disney's Animal Kingdom is his fourth book published by Theme Park Press. The others are *On the Disney Beat*, *An American in Disneyland Paris*, and *Disney's Dream Weavers*. He also collaborated with former Disney cast member Ted Kellogg on his book *Passport to Pixie Dust*.

Since 2009, Chuck has shared his passion for all things Disney in his *Goofy About Disney* blog on SILive.com. He also writes a blog for AllEars.net called *Still Goofy About Disney*.

Chuck resides in Beachwood, New Jersey, with his wife, Janet. They have three adult children and six grandchildren.

ABOUT THEME PARK PRESS

Theme Park Press publishes books primarily about the Disney company, its history, culture, films, animation, and theme parks, as well as theme parks in general.

Our authors include noted historians, animators, Imagineers, and experts in the theme park industry.

We also publish many books by first-time authors, with topics ranging from fiction to theme park guides.

And we're always looking for new talent. If you'd like to write for us, or if you're interested in the many other titles in our catalog, please visit:

www.ThemeParkPress.com

• •

Theme Park Press Newsletter

Subscribe to our free email newsletter and enjoy:

- ♦ Free book downloads and giveaways
- ♦ Access to excerpts from our many books
- ♦ Announcements of forthcoming releases
- ♦ Exclusive additional content and chapters
- ♦ And more good stuff available nowhere else

To subscribe, visit www.ThemeParkPress.com, or send email to newsletter@themeparkpress.com.

Read more about these books
and our many other titles at:

www.ThemeParkPress.com

Printed in Great Britain
by Amazon

20700353R00108